Counselling in Schools –
a Reader

Counselling in Schools – a Reader

Edited by
Keith Bovair and Colleen McLaughlin

David Fulton Publishers
London

David Fulton Publishers Ltd
2 Barbon Close, London WC1N 3JX

First published in Great Britain by
David Fulton Publishers, 1993

Note: The right of the editors to be identified as the editors of this work has been
asserted by them in accordance with the Copyright, Designs and Patents Act
1988.

British Library Cataloguing in Publication Data

A catalogue record for this book is available from the British Library

ISBN 1-85346-224-1

Typeset by RGM Associates, Southport
Printed in Great Britain by BPCC Journals, Exeter

Contents

To our fathers – Peter and La Verne

CONTRIBUTORS

BRIGID PROCTOR is a member of the British Association for Counselling working group which is exploring the role of counselling in education. She is a trained counsellor and well known counsellor trainer, who has published widely on counselling.

PETER LANG is a Senior Lecturer in Education at the University of Warwick, having been a primary teacher for seven years. He has a major interest in affective education and personal and social education both nationally and internationally. His research interests concern teacher, parent and pupil perspectives, with particular reference to the caring dimension of the school's work. His current work also involves seeking ways in which schools may promote the self-esteem and personal and social development of their pupils and staff through the creation and maintenance of whole school policies. He has edited two books on pastoral care and personal and social education and is Features Editor of the journal *Pastoral Care in Education*.

COLLEEN McLAUGHLIN is Tutor in Personal and Social Education at the University of Cambridge Institute of Education, where she runs courses in counselling and personal and social education. She has been a secondary school teacher and an advisory teacher for guidance and counselling. She has edited two books in the field of personal/social education and advisory work. Her research and teaching interests are in the field of affective education and personal/social education. She is also Deputy Editor of *The Curriculum Journal*.

KEITH BOVAIR is currently Headteacher at Durants School, Enfield. He was formerly a lecturer at the University of Birmingham. He has worked extensively in the field of special education in the United Kingdom and in the United States of America. He has published widely in this area.

NEIL HALL, a chartered psychologist, is at present Senior Psychologist for Birmingham Social Services Department and Associate Tutor to the professional training course in educational psychology at the University of Birmingham. He is currently undertaking doctoral research into children's understanding of their memory of traumatic events, with a specific focus upon the development of repression.

GRAHAM UPTON is Professor and Pro Vice-Chancellor at the University of Birmingham. He has taught in ordinary and special schools and has been involved in teacher education for many years. The author of numerous articles on emotional and behavioural problems in schools, he is a former editor of *Maladjustment and Therapeutic Education* and the *Newsletter of the Association for Child Psychology*.

MURRAY WHITE, an ex-primary headteacher in Cambridgeshire, has over the last five years undertaken a training in human relations and become very interested in the development of self-esteem. He recently undertook a secondment from teaching to explore the development of Magic Circle work in primary schools and has published some of his results.

CHARLES MEAD is headteacher of St Paul's Community School, Birmingham. The school exists for pupils who have experienced a wide range of difficulties within mainstream schooling. He has recently completed a city-wide evaluation of peer support group training on recommendations made in the Elton Report.

PAUL TIMMINS, a chartered educational psychologist, is currently Associate Tutor to the Masters degree course in Educational Psychology at the University of Birmingham and is a senior Psychologist in the Educational Psychology Service, Solihull.

PREFACE

This book is intended to be a reader on current practice in counselling in education, and each chapter is introduced by a short summary. The topics and themes which are contained here are ones which are of current interest or which arise out of recent development projects in the field in which the contributors have played a major part. The aim is to be of practical help to teachers working in schools and to further the debate about the place and practice of counselling in schools in the 1990s and beyond. The contributors are all practitioners who are involved in the field either as developers, trainers or teachers.

Theoretical stances contained in the chapters vary and are made explicit, although all contributors are working within a humanistic framework. The book explores work in the primary, secondary and special school settings and focuses on the current state of counselling, its application in schools and some of the ethical and practical considerations arising from the work. Some specialist areas are explored such as peer support and working with abused children. The book will be of interest to those who are working at all levels in counselling in schools: from those who have small involvement and interest to those who are involved in specialist work or the development of practice in schools.

Colleen McLaughlin
Keith Bovair
Cambridge, 1993.

CHAPTER 1

An Overview of Counselling in Britain Today

Brigid Proctor

In this chapter Brigid Proctor gives a comprehensive overview of counselling in Britain in the 1990s, including a description of the explosion of interest in this field. She explores the assumptions and values underlying the practice of counselling, as well as the different uses of counselling and counselling skills. She describes attempts at collective self-discipline in the counselling world and the political and economic context. Finally, she looks briefly at patterns emerging from the overview, including a discussion of the work of the British Association for Counselling.

An overview objectifies. It encourages looking down from a distance. It removes you from the messiness of personal experience, human interaction, organisational and institutional politics, social privilege and deprivation. It sociologises political and economic passion; philosophical and ideological angst; professional rivalry, achievement or failure; spiritual fulfilment or malaise.

In contrast, the activity of counselling has developed in a subjective way. It is usually undertaken by people who are enmeshed in all that messiness. Often they feel passionately about the need for enabling help to be available to those in distress. They have clear and urgent views of the disabling nature of many of our social institutions and

1

practices. 'Counselling' has been more a movement than a practice, developing haphazardly in response to need or where individuals and groups have been moved or inspired by ideas or beliefs. Such differing inspiration has often meant that it has been hard for those people to talk to each other as allies rather than as rivals. In addition, by its nature, 'counselling' has been counter-cultural. Any attempt to look and plan objectively for the provision of counselling on a wide scale has usually been made at the time and expense of the counsellors. They have seldom if ever (except perhaps in relation to AIDS and HIV) had the economic and political clout or backing to carry plans forward in a single sector, let alone across sectors. So an overview will be difficult to offer and may, perhaps, be misleading. Nor will my overview be objective. I have views, thoughts, feelings, doubts, satisfactions and biases which will inevitably influence my picture of the counselling scene.

Dissemination and professionalisation

As a counselling skills trainer, I have been energetically associated with what I would call the disseminating and empowering sector of the counselling movement. Having trained and worked in social work, I have always known that counselling as a structured opportunity for one person to be helped by another was available for very few people. My enthusiasm has gone into sharing counselling ideas and practice with people who, in their day-to-day work, can offer a facilitative relationship to very many people undergoing transitions and crises. I believed that most people had some capacity to be enabling for others, and that they could develop those skills and attitudes with systematic help. Through those years, I came to realise that our culture has been dismal in developing our ability for 'helpful' responses, and that the hierarchical nature of our social relationships is very insidious. In other words, a lot of *unlearning* needed to happen in counselling skills training. My faith that very many people are potentially able to be more helpful to others at times of choice, change, confusion or distress was justified.

Throughout 17 years as a trainer, I had been involved with the British Association for Counselling. On retiring early, I spent three years as Chair of the BAC Training Committee, where I had the opportunity, with others, to think about the wider issues of counselling training. Also, as part of my freelance practice, in partnership, I developed training for counselling supervisors, and for

supervisors of those using counselling skills in their work. In these
roles, I was engaged with the more professionalising arm of the
movement. I came, rather reluctantly, to acknowledge that the
counselling world had to take responsibility for its own standards of
practice. Reluctantly, because I understand the process of
professionalisation to be unintentionally alienating. In working to live
creatively with this tension – the value of 'skills for all' within a framework of responsible thought and practice; alongside increasing
counsellor regulation – I feel like a 'counselling system' in microcosm.

So, bearing in mind the haphazard picture, and my own
involvements, I have chosen to concentrate, in this personal overview,
on:

● the explosion of interest in counselling; both on the part of the
   general public and 'human service professionals';
● the assumptions and values underlying the practice of
   counselling;
● counselling and counselling skills – definitions and distinctions;
● the growth of collective self-discipline in the counselling world;
● politics and economics – the changing pattern of counselling
   provision;
● a brief, fresh look at patterns emerging from this overview.

1 The explosion of interest in counselling

The public

In the last twenty years, the attitude of the general public to
counselling and psychotherapy has changed dramatically. In the 1970s
most people connected the 'need for counselling' with failure, and
mental illness. Alternatively, it smacked of American self-indulgence
and navel gazing. Now, radio, television and the agony aunts all
publicise counselling as a useful resource. Newspapers, and even
Which?, survey different kinds of therapeutic help and occasionally
warn against it. Disaster reporting is accompanied by requests for, or
reports of, counselling support for survivors and relatives. The
increase of telephone help-lines is largely welcomed by press and
public.

All this marks a cultural shift in attitudes to dependency and
independence; and in the delineation of failure and non-coping. It also
marks an acceptance that people can no longer rely on the extended

4

family and familiar community in times of crisis or distress. In acknowledging that vacuum, it seems less bizarre that people should turn to informed strangers for help – among others 'the counsellors'.

The shift has been supported by a new language that makes it seem acceptable to suffer psychologically. The minting of the word 'stress' to cover all sorts of behaviour which would formerly have been called weakness, break down, nerves, and so on, has enabled some people to relate less judgmentally to their own and other people's emotional and social difficulties. By the emphasis on stress and tension as the inter-action of physiology and environment, there is a lifting of personal blame which formerly prevented the more puritanical among us from acknowledging the fear or actuality of not coping well enough. 'Being stressed' brought personal and social difficulties out of the realm of psychiatry as surely as some of the former clinical language of counsellors and psychotherapists had sealed it in.

In parallel, the alternative health movement has stressed the holistic nature of body/mind/spirit health or malaise. This movement seems to have tapped our culture's more romantic/existential aspirations in a way that counselling and psychotherapy on their own could not. In an unpublished paper, Lago (1991) quotes an anthropological 'healing quadrant' (Tseng and Hu, 1979) incorporating four modes of healing which it is suggested are available in all societies. (Figure 1.1)

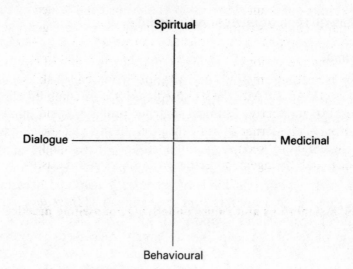

Figure 1.1   An anthropological healing quadrant (after Tseng and Hu, 1979)

Perhaps the current call for counselling bespeaks the hunger for being in a 'moving' and significant dialogue. In addition, counsellors are aware of hopes and expectations of magical, or spiritual release; and tread the boundary between the medicinal and the behavioural and dialogue modes, all of which may fall within their sphere.

Human service professionals

Those who work in what could broadly be called the 'human services' now recognise that there is an activity called counselling; that there are associated communication skills which can be named counselling skills. And they want them. Such professionals are realising that

● interpersonal skills
● self-awareness;
● an understanding of the dynamics of personal change, and
● a framework for thinking about social systems

were largely lacking in their own training.

Moreover, the increased stress under which such workers find themselves leads them to hope that somewhere there is a less stressed corner where, as at least a temporary 'counsellor', they can offer individuals or groups some asylum from intolerable pressures. People who are called counsellors, health professionals or clergy are not alone in the healing quadrant. More people are helped and healed by chance or regular encounters with a loving teacher or wise manager than ever 'go for counselling'.

This is an impressionistic analysis, but the explosion of counselling courses is real. From short introductory counselling skills courses through to MAs and MScs in Counselling or Counselling Psychology, they proliferate yearly. Demand matches provision, and applicants come from every corner of the education, health and social services; from the voluntary sector, the churches and, increasingly, from the personnel and management sectors of business and industry.

2   The assumptions and values underlying counselling practice

Thumbnail history

The skills and awareness which are taught under the name of 'counselling' are based on a comprehensive set of assumptions and values. These are not exclusive to 'the counselling movement', but are shared by many people in their day-to-day lives, both private and professional. They are basically humanistic, and fall into the category of romantic rather than puritan. However, the counselling movement has been responsible for working those values and assumptions into an increasingly coherent practice based on ever more clearly defined skills and attitudes.

Counselling was first heard of in Britain in the 1950s, the National Marriage Guidance Council probably offering the first regular practitioners. Psychotherapy was already well-known. Stemming from the psychoanalysis of Freud and his early colleagues, it was based on European values and experience. It would be a caricature to sketch these as resulting in a practice which was somewhat introverted, hierarchical, and pessimistic/depressive in style – but not a totally unrecognisable caricature. For the most part, it was viewed by professionals and public alike as somewhat marginal and mystical, and it required a long and expensive training. (However, it was a powerful 'aunt Sally' and behavioural and humanistic psychology derived a lot of energy from being 'anti psychoanalysis'.)

Social casework, the predecessor of counselling in the social work field, was derived directly from psychodynamic principles. It was available for the socially disabled, as psychotherapy was mostly for the 'sick'. Some social work training included many of the elements now offered in counselling training, but it was available to social work trainees only.

However, it took two largely American imports to fuel the explosion of response to 'counselling'. One was successive packages of varied humanistic psychotherapies. To caricature these would be to sketch them as extrovert, democratic/charismatic and optimistic/manic. The other was the import of a practice developed out of mainstream academic psychology, which was first purely behavioural, but which is developing into cognitive/behavioural/emotive counselling or therapy. A caricature of that practice might depict pragmatism, relentless realism, and didactic cheerfulness.

Shared legacy

So what are the shared values and assumptions in a counselling movement fed by such diverse tributaries? Put simply, the basic proposition might be *that it is difficult for children, and subsequently adults, to be themselves.* They may not act in ways that meet their fundamental needs, and they may not know how to. One way these needs have been described is:

- to love and be loved;
- to feel powerful for oneself and others and to be able to enjoy proper dependence;
- to be creative and to participate socially with others in creative activity.

Caretakers of children have themselves often been imbued with limited or even mistaken ideas about these needs. They may have had to deny some or all of them for themselves. They therefore pass on strategies and provide environments that encourage 'fitting in'. It is desirable for children to be able to relate with and respond to their changing environments – personal, social, physical – purposefully and flexibly. However, an anxious preoccupation with 'fitting in' exacts a cost. Children may lose the freedom to explore ways of developing emotionally, physically, socially and spiritually *within their own sense of the world and with their own unique resourcefulness*.

This freedom is best experienced when children feel sufficiently loved and valued, and when they can recognise clear and consistent enough edges to their freedom – realistic boundaries and expectations. This self-regarding development provides the sense of worth which makes for loving and being loved. It builds a realistic sense of personal power which allows the child to relax into compliance and dependence, without fearing loss of control or identity. It nurtures the unquenchable creativity of the child, and seems to encourage the ability to enjoy and care about other people if 'cultural messages' suggest this as a value.

The young of any species are hardy and determined, and most parents are, in Winnicot's (1965) description 'good enough'. Most children survive in Britain at present, both physically and with some sense of personal identity. Often they do so using stress-driven strategies that are relatively inflexible. That is, they are motivated by, for example, the need to reduce fear or anxiety, or to avoid a sense of shame, impotence or rage. At times of choice and change in their lives they may have difficulty knowing where to look, or what to do, or how to make sense of the situation they find themselves in. At times of added difficulty which causes them distress or confusion, they may easily find themselves (or tell themselves that they are) unable to cope. The sensations and emotions they experience may be overwhelming and, since as children these responses may have been discouraged, they 'don't know what to do with themselves'.

The counselling process and ethos presumes that if, at that stage, some person who is not over-involved in the outcome of the situation can be at hand, they can be helpful. Counsellors believe that such help needs to provide the kind of facilitative environment which children needed in the first place to survive and flourish. To quote from a paper produced by BAC with the aim of influencing professional bodies in the human service arena:

> People thrive best when they are respected and personally understood; and when they are treated genuinely and encouraged to respond similarly.
>
> We also assume that they have the right and responsibility to engage actively in the processes of their own personal, social and educational development; in the maintenance of their own health and in the amelioration of their own illness or disability.

Carl Rogers (1961) suggested that such a 'not overinvolved person' (or facilitator) needed to offer:

- unconditional respect;
- non-possessive warmth;
- genuineness;
- a continuous and visible (or audible!) engagment with the task of empathic understanding of the highly personal meaning of the client's communication and experience.

Most of us have developed ways of meeting our needs that are counter-productive (such strategies have been called 'unwanted skills'). For instance, assertiveness training has been developed to help people who have learned very well to please others – undoubtedly a useful ability but, in so doing, they have prevented themselves from learning how to be appropriately powerful and creative in their own way. A facilitative environment may often challenge people to unlearn before they relearn.

Some people may have developed such rigid and counter-productive strategies that the word 'therapeutic' is appropriate to the help they may need. (This is also true of some areas of the experience of most of us who usually think of ourselves as 'good copers'.) The inability to cope with the demands of their lives may result from deep and lasting psychic wounds to spirit and identity. Energy is directed, often in ways of which they are largely unaware, to protecting themselves from the pain of those wounds and from the fear of being rewounded. If people feel impelled by distress to address such issues, it is generally agreed that the helping or healing process will have to be profound – which may sometimes equate to long. Facilitators, whatever the name and nature of their professional role, will need to have special skill and understanding if they are to stay empathic and genuine. Moreover they will need some developed self-knowledge in order not to become inappropriately invasive or depriving. Freire (1976) construed that most of us have been both *deprived* (of the love or freedom to develop in our own way) and *invaded* (in the interest of learning and doing what we 'ought'). Unhelpful 'helpers' can further confuse and depower people who, in their distress, can be vulnerable and indiscriminating.

Differing emphases

Although I believe that the assumptions and values I have spoken of would be largely agreed on by all counsellors, there is less consensus about the best way to practice. Practitioners from differing heritages may feel more identity with like minded colleagues than with the 'counselling movement'.

For **client-centred** workers, offering Rogers' (1961) 'core conditions' – the personalised engagement and the freedom from external judgement – is sufficient to help someone come to their own good sense of their situation, and to their own best solutions. **Psychodynamic** practitioners place their faith in the client gaining insight into the way early 'faulty' patterns of relating affect them in the present. Through the medium of the 'therapeutic relationship' they encourage clients to re-experience old hurts and difficulties, and by 'working them through' in that different relationship, come to be freed from them. **Humanistic** counsellors and therapists may place faith in the client becoming more alive to their feelings and sensations 'here and how'; and to the unregarded inner world of visualisation, fantasy, myth and symbol. **Cognitive** counsellors concentrate on the disabling 'messages' clients give themselves and the inappropriate cognitive maps they are using as they seek to live resourcefully. **Behaviourists** place faith in teaching and helping clients to act more appropriately in the world, believing that their hearts and minds will follow.

Increasingly, counsellors from different 'models' or 'schools' are creating approaches which have more regard to the need, context and nature of the client than merely to do 'what I do and how I do it'. At best, such practice is integrative, based on core understanding, beliefs and assumptions which can be worked out flexibly in response to *this*

10

client. At worst, such practice is hit or miss – 'I feel like trying such and such I've just been learning'.

Meanwhile, any (scarce) research available continues to show that effectiveness depends on the 'who' who does it more than the 'what' that is done. Rogers' ingredients for a good enough counsellor – respectfulness; warmth; genuineness; and the ability to convey accurate empathy – have yet to be disproved.

3 Counselling and counselling skills

The counselling task

In the last 20 years, the institutional representative for counselling has been the BAC (which is called British Association for *Counselling*, not counsellors). The definition of counselling that was created in 1985 is still the official definition. Many people in the counselling world use other descriptions as carefully crafted to imply or avoid 'political' implications.

> People become engaged in counselling when a person occupying regularly or temporarily the role of counsellor offers, or agrees *explicitly* to offer, time, attention and respect to another person or persons temporarily in the role of client; in order that the client may have an opportunity to explore, discover and clarify ways of living more resourcefully and towards greater well-being. (BAC, 1985)

In a critical article in *Counselling* (the BAC Journal, August 1992), Alex Howard pointed out that this definition specifies a very vague task, and avoids any mention of how it is done – thereby allowing some shared professional identity to often disagreeing practitioners. What it does identify, however, is that counselling is *a clearly contracted activity, in which the needs and wishes of the 'client' are the agenda*. While this does not distinguish it from the related, and many would say identical, practice of psychotherapy, it does distinguish it from what BAC calls 'using counselling skills'.

Using counselling skills

The 'micro skills' of helping communication have been (almost) definitively identified in the last ten years. Perhaps Gerard Egan (1986) in his much re-edited *Skilled Helper* has been the most influential co-ordinator and definer of micro skills. As a framework, he offers a down-to-earth and integrative description of the 'skilled helping process' which cuts across the preoccupation with role-name or specified task of the helper.

His first and perhaps most accessible formulation of that process was:

- first, explore, with the client, the facts and meanings of what is problematic for him (the client-centred legacy);
- this leads the client into the possibility of developing deeper understanding (the psychodynamic/humanistic/cognitive legacy);
- out of which can emerge client goals and plans for acting (the cognitive/behavioural legacy).

Each stage of the helping process requires the development of specific abilities on the part of the helper, and significantly on the part of the client. These in turn can be broken down into micro-skills for ease and accessibility of learning. For instance, helper abilities that usually need practice are:

- in stage one: the art of empathically, respectfully, tentatively and appropriately reflecting back the content and meaning of the client's words and unspoken messages;
- in stage two: the art of encouraging people to challenge themselves;
- in stage three: stimulating people to think daringly and creatively of their possibilities for action.

In counterpoint, clients need to develop their ability:

- to talk-to-explore (as opposed to the many other purposes of conversation);
- to be open to challenge;
- to be creative.

So, if the helping process is generic, how does 'using counselling skills' differ from 'being temporarily in role of counsellor'? The current working consensus is that it is the explicit contract (or working agreement) which is crucial. A worker may be:

(1) employing some intentional combination of the micro skills above, while
(2) working out of the counselling assumptions and values which I described earlier; but, the task will be

12

(3)   for helper and client (patient, student, worker etc.) to reach an outcome *which is not, or not solely, the client's agenda*

Thus a manager can use counselling skills, to manage in a 'person respecting way'; a year head can use counselling skills when confronting a student with behaviour beyond the limits; a nurse can use counselling skills while teaching a patient how to manage a stoma.

> People often enter training with ability and enthusiasm for relating well to other people. These skills must not be lost as workers develop professionally; they need to be maintained and built on. It demands considerable sensitivity and skill for developing professionals to manage a growing number of tasks and responsibilities and still retain the human touch, in role and under stress.
>
> Since all developing workers are themselves in the role of student and often also feel without skill and lacking in power, they too have the right to be treated with respect, to be supported and challenged in their learning in a way that increases their self-esteem and encourages them to respect themselves, each other and the people to whom they offer a service. (BAC, 1985)

These paragraphs encapsulate what BAC wishes to encourage all 'human service professionals' to experience as part of their training. Significantly, BAC has recently been instrumental in encouraging the DfE to develop a Lead Body for Counselling, Guidance, Advising and Befriending, in order to develop National Vocational Qualifications in these activities. Hopefully, this will lead to the development of agreed building blocks of skills and values which can be validated across sectors, at all levels of pre- and post-professional development. This is the dissemination process to which many counsellors are deeply committed – the use of counselling skills in the promotion of health, learning, self-management and development.

4   Collective self-discipline in the counselling world

Behind the increasingly public face which it offers to the world, BAC has been engaging in highly energetic processes. As an Association it seeks to combine the perceptions and interests of:

- increasingly professional and professionalised counsellors, both employed and freelance;
- voluntary counselling organisations and part-time and volunteer counsellors; and

- those who do not aspire to be 'counsellors' but who want to employ a counselling approach and counselling skills in the work they do with people in a wide variety of settings.

Throughout, it has kept central the concern for the creation and dissemination of competent ethical practice. With this in mind, it has created Codes of Ethics for counsellors, people using counselling skills, supervisors and trainers. It has published information sheets on a wide variety of subjects, as well as putting out more substantial publications. It has, in the search for standards, offered Accreditation to adequately qualified and experienced counsellors, Recognition to experienced and competent supervisors, and shortly, to counselling trainers. It sets and maintains high standards for the Recognition of substantial counsellor trainings, and is exploring how to set and maintain standards for substantial counselling skills trainings. It offers directories of counsellors, trainings and counselling services. It has a developed complaints procedure. Through its Divisions, it offers opportunities for those with common interests to associate; and through local branches it offers support for local networking.

Protection of the public

The major overt motivation in creating these complex, expensive and time-consuming developments has been the protection of the public from exploitation, and from irresponsible and incompetent practice. BAC has worked hard to inform the consumer as well as to make clear demands of its member practitioners. My personal opinion is that these demands of themselves have, hearteningly, raised standards of practice.

Unfortunately, as in other professions, consistent consumer protection is not possible – charlatans and egotists seem marvellously equipped to jump any hurdle laid in their path. Many see the work done by BAC as not good enough. For instance Accreditation for counsellors, at present, is based on the paper representation of hours and content of training and practice. All newer developments are financed out of the pockets of members, and mostly undertaken virtually voluntarily. Moreover, the differences in approach, discussed earlier, mean that any consensus in standards has to be suitably vague if it is to be inclusive.

Restrictive practice

Simultaneously, these achievements are seen by others as a massive lurch towards professionalisation and counsellor restrictive practices. The raising of standards of training and of supervision requirements has economic consequences (which will be apparent in the next section).

The creation of the European Community has underlined the grain of truth in the accusations of restrictive practices. As a direct result of that pressure, both the psychotherapists and the counselling psychologists have formed themselves into separate professional bodies in an attempt to find common ground for Registration. Effort is now going (with as yet little success) into usefully distinguishing between counselling and psychotherapy; and many people who see counselling as their career are feeling the need to get degrees in Counselling Psychology or to undertake psychotherapy training. This leads those who do not wish to do this, or who might not be eligible or economically able, to fear that counsellors will become a poor relation of psychotherapists or counselling psychologists. Worse, they might be barred from practising.

The explosion of books on counselling, and of long and short courses on general and particular skills and issues, suggests a richness of resource. It also triggers feelings, in established workers in the field, of being undertrained, deskilled and alienated. It seems a long way from the volunteer roots of much original counselling.

5   Politics and economics – access to counselling

So much for the internal world of counselling – a providers' perspective. Meanwhile, the wider economic and political climate is not in synchronisation with the increased public demand for counselling and counselling training. Access for consumers to counselling in the public and voluntary sectors has not commensurately increased – a consumers' perspective. Moreover, the pattern of provision has changed in some interesting ways.

The public sector

School counsellors seem to have come and very largely gone; the rest of this book will be concerned with how counselling and schools now relate. The provision of specialist counsellors (or alternatively student service officers who counsel) in Further Education appears to be patchy and largely under threat. The number of counsellor hours does not keep step with student hours.

Similarly, counsellors in Higher Education establishments are under increasing strain. Institutions are obliged to take in higher numbers of students and more of those have difficulty with the academic and social demands of HE. Under economic pressure, too, student services are at best maintained, and are usually under threat. Nevertheless some universities and polytechnics do still have established Counselling Services which have managed to hold their own. They may be associated with Student Health Services, or be independent services. In general, however, the provision of counselling in education has not mirrored the increase in counselling training, public demand or student numbers.

In the Health Services, too, it is difficult to see that there is increased provision, despite the greatly increased numbers of workers who do some counselling training. General Practice rules have changed to allow counsellors to be employed in GP practices and this is a growth area for counselling. In some practices, too, private counsellors have an arrangement with GPs. However, the small number of hours likely to be offered means that demand almost always outstrips supply.

In hospitals, 'counselling' can usually only be offered by clinical psychologists or, in some instances, psychotherapists or social workers. In any case, it is an extremely scarce resource. Community psychiatric services often have specialist nurses with counselling training; and may have clinics where counselling is offered. Health visitors, too, are sometimes in a position to offer limited formal counselling to their patients. Speech, occupational and physio-therapists were beginning to offer counselling to some of their patients and patient relatives. They are now under so much pressure that they are unlikely to be able to continue. Outpatient clinics, Child Guidance Units, Family Centres etc. have certainly not increased in number or provision.

The statutory Social Services are under such economic pressure, and have such increased statutory responsibilities, that there are fewer and fewer 'corners' where individual or group case-work/counsel-ling/therapy is available.

The voluntary sector

There is a wide variety of organisations, large and small, local and national, offering counselling and related services. All of them are competing for the same scarce funds. Subsidies for Youth Counselling

Centres have been cut. Specialist agencies such as Relate or Cruse (relationship and bereavement counselling respectively) which have national and regional organisation are in economic crisis, with the same increased demand from clients and from trainees.

Relate now has a fully professionalised structure for the training, support and management of its volunteer counsellors – a very expensive business. The same is true of the Catholic Marriage Advisory Council and, for instance, Cruse is developing in that direction. As a direct result of increased professionalisation, it is considered that it is not 'good enough' to allow people of goodwill to act as counsellor to others out of the goodness of their heart. (They may after all, the belief goes, be doing it more for themselves than for others. What, one might ask, about well paid professionals?) So the legitimate and necessary concern for standards and accountability leads to heavier organisation and longer training, which in turn prices the old kind of volunteer counselling out of the market. Clients of Relate are now expected to pay for services according to their means. Nevertheless, it is one of the few agencies still offering access to counselling for people with low incomes.

There has been a proliferation of specialist organisations where people with shared concerns around a specific illness, disability or social circumstance may be offered help and support. This may be called befriending, or 'a talk with our contact person', or it may be called counselling. It may or may not be a clearly contracted purposeful, confidential interaction which falls within the BAC definition. Such organisations have a wealth of specialist understanding around, for example, eating disorders, single parenthood, schizophrenia, cancer, asthma, or parenting. If they choose to move along the counselling path, they are faced with providing training, management, support and supervision, all of which make increased economic and organisational demands.

In addition to such specialist help and/or counselling services, there are some general counselling services, serving a specific locality. Often starting as free and volunteer services, they are caught in the same squeeze; some still have the freedom to offer subsidised fees, but their standard fees equate with those of private practitioners.

The private sector

Private counselling and psychotherapy practice is proliferating, in response to the increased demand. Although some practitioners will operate a sliding scale, many do not. Fees per hour (or 50 mins) are anything from £15–£45. BAC offers a limited safeguard to consumers by publishing a directory of counsellors and psychotherapists. Entrants must subscribe to an organisation which requires them to adhere to a Code of Ethics. This offers clients the possibility of making a formal complaint to the relevant organisation if they believe their practitioner has infringed it. So counselling may be more available in the private sector, but usually for the well-enough heeled.

The workplace

The other sector where counselling opportunities for all are expanding is the workplace. While the human services continue to respond to the counselling ethos as if it were some sort of indulgent frill, the business community has understood its usefulness. (To be realistic, this is often prompted by the horror of dealing with extensive redundancies.) Many large organisations now offer counselling through Staff Counsellors, or through contracted Employee Assistance Programmes. Here, time and money are important, and it appears that really effective work is being done in a short-term focused way, incorporating such 'person centred behavioural work' as stress management, assertion training, etc.

Multi-cultural and multi-ethnic access *

Meanwhile the development of a multi-cultural and multi-ethnic society is challenging counselling trainers to notice how culture bound are their ideas and practices. The humanistic assumptions can be oppressive to clients from different cultures and sub-cultures. They may come hoping for advice, guidance, family negotiation; or some clear understanding of persecutory experiences, or cross-cultural dilemmas. Some counsellors offer them insight and interpretation. The provision of counsellors from Asian and Afro-Caribbean communities is unequal to the demand; and such provision is tied up with access to training, and relevant training.

Many courses, even those in large multi-ethnic urbanisations, spend little time in exploring cross-cultural attitudes to 'helping'. Counselling centres and courses are often not aware of how unappealing they appear to non-white clients or students. The training budgets of both public and voluntary sectors have been drastically cut and students are more typically expected to pay their own costs. What were subsidised training courses are now usually full cost (and, of course, most privately offered training has always been so). This directly affects, for instance, local agencies sending volunteers on Further Education counselling courses, and defeats good intentions for attracting a wide range of counsellors.

6 Patterns emerging

Composing this complex overview, I have often felt pessimistic. The forces affecting the counselling movement seemed beyond the control of individuals or pressure groups – political ideology, economics, the subtle pull into hierarchical professionalism, erosion and exploitation, in the public services, of generosity and goodwill. By focusing and exploring themes, I found my attitude changing.

From private belief to public acceptance

No one would have believed, twenty years ago, that counselling would have emerged from the closet, and have been welcomed and accepted in many areas of public life.

Humanistic assumptions have entered public consciousness. We are more emotionally literate than we used to be. People do understand more about how they work, and what happens between people. The language and development of 'social skills' is more acceptable (if sometimes depressingly functional). When I heard that elementary school children in the USA were being helped to be 'pro-actively [that is, choicefully and within their own sense of values] assertive, aggressive [in the sense of interventionist], and compliant', I felt that could not happen here. Now, I am not so sure – if the syllabus allowed. In training and in counselling people discover that they are hooked on their stress-driven strategies; and that they need to unhook themselves in order to develop flexibility. How useful if they could be helped earlier, before they were hooked.

Dissemination

Counselling skills training continues to be a growth industry and, with the development of NVQs, dissemination is irreversible and access assisted. Many trainers are keen to use the materials available; to work within the trainers' Code of Ethics; and to be aware of where their courses fit with others offered; and students are quite well informed consumers.

Stepping stones

Counselling skill is progressive. 'It seemed to be the first time she felt anyone really listened to her, and I was quite overwhelmed by what she told me about herself.' To continue to be helpful beyond that point requires personal resources and developing sensitivity and skill. Two typical resources are long or short term further training; and the kind of facilitative support, challenge and monitoring which only like-minded colleagues can offer. In counselling terminology, this is supervision. (See the BAC Code of Ethics for People using Counselling Skills.)

Networks not hierarchies

To date, the counselling world has been quite good at resisting hierarchies. The ability to create a working alliance which engages the whole person of 'the other' is widespread – most clients (I hope) feel related to as 'proper adults', even if they are distressed or feeling childish. This is notable, too, in counselling supervision. Supervisor and counsellor usually relate as colleagues, rather than 'expert and novice'.

This leads me to hope that, with the development of increased professionalisation and longer trainings, what will emerge is a *network*. More highly trained counsellors will act as nodes in the network, offering initial and on-going training; supervision, consultation and research. At the grass-roots, workers will adapt practice to their clientele, and feed this back into the training system. In this way, life-long development need not mean losing the human touch, and research and practice can be mutually useful.

Integration and focused work

Cross-fertilisation between different schools of practice is now well established. Both pressure of economics and increased consumer awareness help in this respect. Workers and clients want counselling to be effective; and that means trawling for effective practice wherever it happens. This emphasis is already breaking up the unofficial hierarchy of 'long-term is proper counselling. I only use counselling skills'. Short term focused work is as akin to the latter as the former.

I am guardedly hopeful that counsellors have sufficient genuineness, empathy, and respect for themselves and their clientele to create their own facilitative environment, and come to their own good sense.

References

Egan, G. (1986) *The Skilled Helper*. Montery: Brooks Cole.

Freire, P. (1976) *Education: the Practice of Freedom*. London: Writers and Readers Publishing Co-operative.

Howard, A. (1992) 'BAC and Accreditation'. *Counselling – Journal of the British Association for Counselling* Vol. 3, No. 3. August, 1992.

Lago, C. (1991) Unpublished paper delivered to Keele University.

Rogers, C. (1961) *On Becoming a Person*. Boston: Houghton Mifflin.

Tseng and Hu (1979) in Marsalla *et al.* (1979) *Culture and Psychotherapy: Perspectives on Cross-cultural Psychology*. New York: Academic Press.

Winnicot, D. W. (1965) *Maturational Processes and the Facilitating Environment*. London: Hogarth Press.

Note: BAC Code of Ethics for People Using Counselling Skills is available along with other BAC material mentioned in this chapter from British Association for Counselling, 1 Regent Place, Rugby CV21 2PJ.

CHAPTER 2

Counselling in the Primary School: an Integrated Approach

Peter Lang

In this chapter Peter Lang argues that in order for counselling to be effective in primary schools we need to take a broader definition of counselling than the traditional one of dealing with pupil problems. The approach needs to be an integrated one. The chapter raises a number of issues related to current perspectives and practice, including the argument that counselling in schools has proactive and pedagogical implications. He discusses what teachers might do to promote an integrated approach.

Introduction

So few parents have the feeling that children are capable people. You know, we just think of them as children, and the concept of children equals inability to deal with life.

Jane said, 'I don't want to go to the playground. The others won't let me join their club. First they say I can and then they say I can't and they change their minds.' I hurt for her but I just said, 'That must be very confusing for you when they can't make up their minds whether they want you in with them or not.' And Jane just said, 'Yes it is. I know what I am going to do. I'm going to start my own club!' (Parents quoted in Sokolov and Hutton, 1988)

Though the quotations above are from parents they highlight two important aspects of the operation of counselling in the primary school: the significance of the perceptions that underlie the process; and that the child's ability to respond is often as important as the adult's skill. I believe issues such as these make it impossible to consider counselling in an individualised vacuum (the child-the problem-the teacher/counsellor-the process). For counselling to be effective in the primary school the broader context in which it operates must be taken into account and it should be integrated into a whole school approach. In the chapter that follows this will be my main concern. Thus, more traditional concerns – the enumeration of pupil problems, the skills for dealing with them, consideration of core personal qualities and issues of professionality – will only be considered as part of this broader approach. This chapter will first raise a number of issues relating to current perspectives and practice, and then go on to suggest a number of things that teachers and schools might do to promote an integrated approach. Such an approach involves issues to do with feelings, emotions and perceptions of self and the personal and social skills closely related to these. These concerns relate to both pupils and teachers and can be seen as falling within the affective as opposed to cognitive educational domain. The approach involves the promotion of effective communication and support and an appropriate organisational style and school climate. The major aim is to enhance the well-being and development of all involved, effective learning being seen as an important part of this. The support of pupils facing problems and difficulties will be much better catered for within such a framework than as a result of a school response purely focused on the problems. Counselling is more easily seen as part of this positive approach if it is recognised as a general communication process as well as something directed to problem solving.

Current perceptions

The case for counselling in the primary school is usually made in terms of the increase in the personal and social difficulties and traumas faced by a growing number of primary pupils. This perspective is the main one taken by a number of the writers who have considered counselling in relation to the primary phase, for example Murgatroyd (1980) and Galloway (1981).

Such an emphasis is to be expected as counselling must be concerned with the problems of the counselled; and the problems found amongst primary school pupils are certainly real, and if not on the increase they are at least being recognised more frequently – the issue of abuse is a good example of this. In a report produced for the Calouste Gulbenkian Foundation, La Fontaine (1991) analysed the case notes of over 2,000 calls to the 'Bullying Line' in a period of nine months; 68 per cent were from children between seven and thirteen.

Again, perhaps not so serious but still significant are the pupil concerns revealed in Measor and Woods' study of the transition from middle to secondary school.

> Pupil anxiety revolved around five major issues: the size and more complex organisation of the new school, new forms of discipline and authority, new demands of work, the prospect of being bullied, and the possibility of losing one's friends. (Measor and Woods, 1984)

The authors note that these concerns encompass both the academic and the social, so that pupils are in effect experiencing a number of different transitions.

I am not seeking to suggest that these clear needs should not be responded to, but that a traditional response conceived mainly in terms of one-to-one counselling may be less than effective, and that an over-emphasis on such a perspective may leave the context in which such a process operates unconsidered. One problem with this approach is that it can come to be seen as a kind of exercise in calibration. Here the common sense view is that it is just a matter of aligning certain sets of skills, or degree of skill with different orders of problems. An example of such a hierarchical perspective is found in the writing of Charlton and Hoye (1987). In a chapter on counselling in the primary school they have provided a well developed and logical gradation which describes three levels of counselling:

Level One
All teachers should be equipped to contribute at this level. This, it is claimed, does not mean that teachers should be fully trained counsellors, but it does imply that all teachers should possess an understanding of and be proficient in using basic counselling skills. They go on to suggest that one of the skills required is teacher vigilance; the ability to be watchful over each child's behaviour and sensitive to changes that take place. Though this takes the notion of counselling beyond the simple one-to-one situation, it is still a fairly passive and individualised approach. Later it will be argued that for pupils to have access to teachers and for teachers to have access to

pupils' feelings, considerably more needs to be done than keeping an eye open.

Level Two

At this level they suggest the severity of the problems presented may necessitate regular and protracted individual counselling sessions for which they feel class teachers usually have neither time nor competence. Here we see a very clear illustration of the way that both problems and skills are seen hierarchically.

Level Three

Problems at this level will be serious enough for referral to outside agencies to be unavoidable and very necessary.

Apart from describing the different levels of counselling, they draw attention to the close relationship between teaching and counselling processes and seek to differentiate between them. They suggest that:

> Counselling can be construed as a teacher response to problems evinced or experienced by pupils. While these responses may also include a teaching element (e.g. where pupils need to learn new inter-personal skills) they are, foremost, a response consequent to the teacher's awareness (through observing or listening) of perceived, or anticipated, pupil problems.

They also argue that counselling skills practised in classrooms can be usefully seen in three differing though related contexts.

(1) In a reactive sense where teachers respond to pupils' problems that they have become aware of, they may work on these themselves or where appropriate refer them to specialised help.

(2) They may be so well integrated within the day-to-day teaching activities that no true separation is discernible between teaching and counselling. While imparting knowledge and information, teachers remain vigilant, and more-or-less immediately responsive, to potential or prevailing problems within their class.

(3) They may be employed in both a planned proactive and reactive sense. Teachers may use counselling techniques, in preference to more formal didactic methods, to promote some aspects of their children's personal and social well being.

In relation to the last category Charlton (1988) reports a number of studies suggesting that the use of counselling skills (loosely defined) can enhance such things as children's reading performance. The view of counselling from which a categorisation such as this is developed is an important one and relates closely to the perspective promoted in this paper.

Broadening the perspective

Charlton and Hoye's categorisation is important for the way that it focuses on the idea that counselling and the skills associated with it go beyond the idea of simply helping pupils with problems, that there are also proactive and pedagogical implications. At this point it is appropriate to provide a definition of counselling which includes the broader approach with which we are concerned.

A definition of counselling

Charlton and Hoye's definition, which has already been quoted, can provide part of what is needed. Here it is seen as a process that takes place either as a result of or in anticipation of a pupil problem. This is, of course, the core of the task of counselling traditionally conceived, but if it is to make a real contribution to the support and development of pupils in school its conception must be broadened. In relation to the role of counselling in the primary school I would suggest that the definition should include

> The process through which teacher and pupil can communicate freely at an individual level on matters falling within the affective domain, i.e. feelings, emotions etc. Though such communication may focus on problems this need not be the case and it may be of a purely positive nature.

Counselling in this definition is also concerned with the learning and organisation involved in creating a situation where teachers and pupils can communicate most effectively one to one or in groups about affective concerns. When the term counselling is used there is likely to be a focus on dealing with problems and providing support, and with a particular type of relationship; possibly also with the idea of a greater need for on-going periods of time when pupil and teacher work together. In the case of counselling skills, though these are used in the counselling situation, they also operate in their own right. They can be concerned with developing communication at an affective level or be seen as part of the teacher's repertoire of teaching skills.

In relation to this point Charlton draws attention to the value of counselling skills.

> Of particular interest are the occasions when these enhancements have been shown to produce associated gains in children's academic performance levels (e.g. Lawrence, 1971; 1972). The simplicity of the counselling skills used in such studies and, in one (Lawrence, 1972), the ease with which lay professionals acquired them, suggests that if elementary skills of this type do not already exist within teachers' skills repertoire, they can easily be incorporated. (Charlton, 1988)

The suggested distinction between counselling and counselling skills is valuable at a political level in that it makes an area of potential threat more acceptable to primary class teachers. Counselling skills can be seen as both less specialised and less demanding. However, it is in some ways a misleading distinction as generally neither counselling without basic skills nor skills without relationships is effective.

Current realities

> The role of personal and social education in the primary school is something that needs careful thought, analysis and planning – yet this is at least partly because PSE is likely to be one of the most 'taken for granted' aspects of what is believed to happen in the primary school. (Lang, 1988)

Though I was writing about personal and social education in the quotation above I believe that very much the same could be said about counselling. It is taken for granted that it happens, but there is little or no reflection about it – the assumption tends to be that class teachers can include a counselling dimension to their work with individual pupils. For example, it is assumed in many schools that class teachers spend much of their time listening to individual pupils. However, extended observation in primary classrooms has shown that often the teacher only spends short spaces of time with pupils individually and that this time is often filled with teacher talk, and even when it comes to talking to pupils in groups this tends to be very much teacher controlled and dominated.

Lewis (1991), writing about special needs, supports the view that teachers do not spend a lot of time with pupils individually.

> Evidence from HMI reports (e.g. DES 1978, 1988) and individual research projects suggest that this kind of activity is rarely found in primary schools. One study of four year olds in school noted:
>
> Diagnosis of children's understandings were very noticeable by their absence, or were limited to brief encounters of an unsatisfactory

kind . . . [teachers] very rarely had to deem a task, or a child a failure, since they were always able to find some aspect acceptable. It follows from this that almost every task could be judged a success, which is precisely what teachers did, irrespective of whether or not the child, or the work, had been seen (Bennett and Kell, 1989: p. 82).

An alternative approach to counselling in the primary school

I have spent some time reviewing the situation both in terms of what tends to be said about counselling at this phase of education and in terms of some of the realities of attitudes and practice in schools. I accepted that many pupils do indeed have the sort of problems that can be helped through a traditional counselling approach and that there are skills through which classroom teachers can respond to their pupils when they recognise that they are in need of help. I do not believe that this actually happens very much and would argue that we are dealing with such complex and closely interrelated factors that simply taking a pupil aside and responding to her or him briefly in a counselling mode is unlikely to be effective. I am not suggesting that teachers should not be ready to handle and respond to disclosure of abuse, offer support in cases of bereavement and help with personal problems generally. It is also important that teachers always operate at a high professional level; a key element of this is offering all pupils a listening and confidential ear, in so far as the latter is possible in relation to the teacher's contractual and legal obligations. I believe that the professionality comes in ensuring that the confidentiality that can be offered is maintained and that all pupils understand what the position is.

Some ways forward

Schools and teachers need to think about and organise things in their own way, a way relevant to their particular situation. However they need a basis on which to work and guidance as to the most effective ways of doing this. The following is a set of suggestions of things that I believe should be done if the promotion of an integrated approach to counselling is to be taken seriously. Much of what is suggested below will contribute to the school's effectiveness in ways far beyond the simple promotion of adequate support for pupils, and this will apply to both the affective and cognitive dimensions.

28

Not taking things for granted

However well a particular primary school may feel it is doing, this does not mean that it is under no obligation to check things out at regular intervals. Both schools as institutions and teachers as individuals tend to feel they know rather more than they often do. Indeed the controversy over testing in the primary school revolves around just such an issue, with teachers convinced they already know how pupils are progressing, and some evidence appearing to show that the systematic tests have encouraged at least some to heighten their expectations of their pupils.

Not taking things for granted means both reflecting on the basis of practice and at the same time examining it. A school concerned to do this in relation to an integrated approach to counselling might first encourage staff to share perceptions and reflect on their own attitudes and feelings. Such a process should ideally be an integral part of the on-going work of a school, for example one primary school I visited recently had set aside every fourth staff meeting for the staff themselves – a time to reflect together, to share and support. When practice is examined, this may be done by staff individually, seeking ways to systematically monitor what they do. Again it may be done on a shared basis in terms of mutual support and observation. However practice is examined, data collected might include time spent with individual pupils, duration of each contact, how much time each individual pupil receives, opportunities given to pupils for discussion, how easily available the teacher is to the child, how easy it is for pupil to speak to teacher without being overheard. Even where a school is concerned solely to help its teachers offer basic counselling to pupils in need, an awareness of what is already happening is still important. If the only contact pupils are used to is limited to relatively frequent but very short interaction with their teacher, and where these interactions mainly involve teacher talk and teacher direction, it is unlikely that pupils will respond in a way that will allow them to benefit from the sudden introduction of a counselling approach.

Perhaps most critical of all is the process of asking the pupils what they think and how they perceive things. This may be done through individual interviews, class discussions and simple questionnaires; where a school has a programme of personal recording (ROAs) the process of 'asking the pupils' can be built into this. Clearly apart from helping the schools understand where they actually are rather than where they think they are, pupil consultation has knock-on effects for pupil perceptions and feelings. The importance of this final process cannot be over-emphasised. My own research has shown again and again that what teachers believe pupils feel and what they actually do feel can be very different (Lang 1985, 1988). On a number of occasions headteachers have stressed to me the contribution of their talks in assembly to their pupils' personal and social development, talks which the pupils say they have found boring and incomprehensible.

Self-awareness

The antidote to taking things for granted lies partly in promoting self-awareness amongst staff, but this also forms the basis for developing an integrated approach to counselling. Once the school has been through the initial stage described above it must seek to ensure that the momentum is not lost. One part of this will be maintaining the process of sharing and reflecting and through this the heightened level of self-awareness. In a number of schools an important part of this has been the development of a school ethos statement or set of common values. The creation of this must be supported by and involve all staff, and can of course provide direction for the school development plan. Such a statement is not static or for all time and thus how it is actually reflected in what happens in the school and its continuing appropriateness can form a basis for the reflective processes with which we are concerned. The nature of an integrated approach to counselling will affect the nature of the statement made. Issues such as confidentiality, child protection and response to disclosure clearly involve both.

At a more personal level it will be very valuable if staff can work together to relate their own feelings and experiences to those of their pupils. They might, for instance, consider their own childhood experiences of being labelled in relation to the current experiences of their pupils and go on to consider ways in which labelling the deed rather than the doer might be promoted. This is another example of how the school's shared values and its integrated approach to counselling might relate to each other. The common values might state that labelling of pupils was unacceptable, the integrated approach involve ways of developing alternative approaches when dealing with pupils' inappropriate behaviour. Developing and maintaining staff self- and group-awareness is fundamental to the type of approach I am advocating; without it individual pupil–teacher interactions will be impoverished and the level of care offered by the school as an institution diminished.

The care of teachers

Where such a process of reflection, sharing, awareness and open communication has been established amongst staff and its maintenance catered for, much that is important in terms of the care of teachers will exist. Staff will feel able to share their worries, reservations and problems and are likely not only to feel but to be supported. Of course this does not relieve those who manage schools of a responsibility for staff well-being. In the first place they need to facilitate and resource the processes that have been described. They will also need to work with their colleagues in a way that makes them feel cared for and listened to; this is of course what is meant by an integrated approach, as those teachers who feel uncared for and unlistened to may respond to pupils in the same way.

Views of the child

Stainton-Rogers (1989), writing about different views of childhood, points out that there are alternative views of the nature of childhood and the potential or indeed right for children to control their own lives; these can range from considering them in effect 'fully adult' to the other extreme where they are seen as a 'protected species'. He goes on to note that how you are treated affects how you will treat others. Teachers' views of children are often one of the most unexamined areas within a school. Clearly the opening up of this issue is central to an integrated approach to counselling. The terms in which the school perceives its pupils must be on the basis of conscious reflection rather than that of unconscious belief, for it will affect all that happens in the school from its overall organisation to the individual counselling encounter. Probably the sort of approach that Stainton-Rogers suggests would be the most meaningful. Here an awareness of the different constructions of childhood available and their pros and cons would be developed and their positive dimensions would inform the view the school develops, a view likely to be articulated in its statement of common values.

Skills and attitudes

These are areas which most traditional discussions of counselling would devote considerable space to but I shall only touch on them briefly. This is because they are more effectively developed through practice and should therefore be part of the school's Inset. Here it is their relationship to the integrated approach with which I am concerned. Research suggests that the qualities that underpin effective counselling are things such as genuineness, warmth and unconditional positive regard. I believe it follows that staff who are involved in a reflective supportive environment are much more likely to offer them to their pupils. Empathy is again a critical skill and the ability to be empathetic with others is closely related to the level of self-awareness a teacher has; here again the integrated approach should provide the necessary conditions for staff to increase their skill. In particular the regular sampling of pupil views and perspectives suggested above will contribute to the level of empathy that teachers can offer, as they will have clearer ideas about how pupils in general feel.

Finally, active listening is of central importance, but in many primary schools it is a fairly problematic area:

> It is rare enough that adults listen to each other, but it almost never happens that adults really pay attention to what a child is telling them; much less take the trouble to enquire about their opinions and points of view. (Sokolov and Hutton, 1988)

Again, though these comments are addressed to parents they apply to many classrooms and staff-rooms. As I have already suggested there is a great deal of fantasy in many primary schools about the amount of listening that is done. Much gets in the way of effective listening, not least teachers' desire to help pupils. Sokolov and Hutton draw attention to what they describe as 'interfer-iority complexes':

> We want so much to help, teach, advise and reassure that it goes against all our instincts to keep quiet and let our children do the talking.

In my experience very many primary teachers suffer from 'interfer-iority complexes' but they are nearly always quite unaware of this.

Thus the first thing that has to be promoted in the development of the skills of active listening is an acceptance that they are needed. This is another example of the need for an integrated approach, for such acceptance is likely to develop through all the processes of analysis, reflection and increasing self-awareness already described.

Again, it is far more likely that teachers who are used to being listened to by colleagues will listen to their pupils.

Of course this does not mean that some basic training is not also needed. Schools will need to seek ways or providing some basic training in the essential skills of active listening. However, even where teachers are equipped with all the necessary skills, how they are able to use these will depend very much on school and classroom organisation and teaching style.

Organistion and the integrated approach

Important features of classroom and school organisation which relate to an integrated approach to counselling have already been touched on in our discussion so far, however there are further specific implications.

Basic to such organisation is the provision of individual contact time for each pupil with their class teacher. Lewis (1991) provides a useful model for this in her excellent book on special needs and the national curriculum:

> Several writers have drawn attention to the importance of teachers 'interviewing' children as they work, to monitor the children's learning strategies. It is important for all children but especially so for children who seem to have difficulty in learning. Various terms have been used for this type of activity, including 'TIC' (Teacher inter-action with the child; Hunter-Carsch, 1990), tutorial dialogue (Meadows and Cashdan, 1988), 'analytic interviews' (Bennett et al., 1984) and diagnostic teaching (e.g. Stott, 1978). I am using the term 'child–adult conference' because this emphasises the two-way sharing of information focusing on a specific activity... Roger Beard (1987) suggests that it would be helpful for teachers to divert time from routinely hearing children read to carrying out less frequent, but more in-depth reading interviews with children. The NC, with its emphasis on continuous teacher assessments, will require the kind of approach advocated by Roger Beard and others. Child–adult conferences are discussed here because they are central to identifying the points in learning that are reached by individual children.

The type of framework that Lewis suggests could form an important element in an integrated approach to counselling. It relates to the National Curriculum and individual learning needs and therefore does not need special justification, but it also gives the pupils the experience of being exclusively listened to and the teachers the opportunity to develop their counselling skills. It would be relatively easy to include an affective dimension to such conferences again, giving pupils the chance to develop the skills of talking about their feelings and the teacher of becoming aware of any problems the pupil has. Such developments would also be possible through work done for the pupil's personal record (ROAs). Should a situation develop where the teacher needs to counsel a pupil in the full sense there will be a much firmer basis on which to do this.

Apart from individual work, there should be regular opportunities for pupils to learn to talk and express their feelings as part of their classroom experience. A particularly effective way of doing this is 'circle time' – see for example Wiltshire County Council (1991) and Murray White's chapter in this book. Here pupils sit in a circle of which the teacher is also a member; there are some agreed ground rules: 'everyone listens', 'no put downs', 'everyone gets a turn', 'no-one has to speak', 'same rules apply to the teacher' and the focus can vary from esteem-raising to discussing a classroom problem. Well used 'circle time' can provide a vehicle for pupils to discuss a wide range of affective topics. There is of course a range of other ways of working with groups of pupils which will achieve similar ends. It is through strategies such as these that pupils gain support from each other and also become more skilled at handling and expressing their feelings and emotions. It might be argued that it is not only teachers who need to develop skills to make counselling as effective as possible.

Whole-school organisation

There is not space to go into the issue of the school's organisation and ethos in detail, but as this provides the context for the integrated approach, it is extremely important. A climate which offers some praise and a lot of encouragement is essential, as is a climate where feelings are recognised and valued, where the positive is highlighted and the inappropriate handled consistently and fairly. Everyone should be involved, not just teachers and pupils. It is important that pupils should be encouraged to contribute to the promotion of climate and organisation in a proactive way, in particular in relation to the creation of the rules upon which the school agrees. There are as many ways through which schools can approach the above as there are for ensuring that no pupil is left out. The important thing is the recognition of the need to consciously address the issues, not the precise manner in which this is done. I have visited a number of schools where such whole-school approaches have been developed to great effect.

Conclusion

In this chapter I have intentionally limited the attention given to the specifics of counselling individual pupils in the primary school. I have done this not because it is unimportant but because a short chapter such as this should have other priorities. It is also important to say that at a practical level even the most basic counselling skills require more than a chapter if there is to be any impact on the actual practice of the reader. My priority has been to highlight the importance of what I have described as an integrated approach to counselling. I have suggested that this means something much broader both in terms of the conception and the way it is developed. My concern has been with meeting the affective needs of both staff and pupils in ways that do not simply respond to crisis but seek to promote the positive well-being of all involved and that of the institution itself. I have argued for an extended view of the counselling process which includes this positive dimension and sought to show that counselling is a vital part of this broader approach, but only a part.

I have tried to present schools with real possibilities, and much of what I have written is based on actual experience. I am aware that many will say 'This is all very well but we simply do not have the time'. My answer to this is that generally where schools are prepared to make a real commitment to the processes described, they end up more effective, problems diminish and life becomes less stressful and easier.

References

Beard, R. (1987) *Developing Reading 3–13*. London: Hodder and Stoughton.
Bennett, N. and Kell, A. (1989) *A good start*. Oxford: Basil Blackwell.
Bennett, N., Desforges, C., Cockburn, A. and Wilkinson, B. (1984) *The Quality of Pupil Learning Experiences*. London: ILEA.
Charlton, T. and Hoye, L. (1987) 'Counselling in the Primary School' in David, K. and Charlton, T. (eds) *The Caring Role of the Primary School*. London: Macmillan Education.

Charlton, T. (1988) 'Using counselling skills to enhance children's personal, social and academic functioning' in Lang, P. (ed) *Thinking...About Personal and Social Education in the Primary School.* Oxford: Basil Blackwell.

DES (1978) *Primary Education in England.* London: HMSO.

DES (1988) *The New Teacher in School.* London: HMSO.

Galloway, D. (1981) *Teaching and Counselling: Pastoral Care in Primary and Secondary schools.* Harlow: Longman.

Hunter-Carsch, M. (1990) 'Learning strategies for pupils with literacy difficulties: motivation, meaning and imagery' in Pumfrey, P.D. and Elliott, C.D. (eds) *Children's Difficulties in Reading, Spelling and Writing.* Basingstoke: Falmer.

La Fontaine, J. (1991) *Bullying: the Child's View.* London: Calouste Gulbenkian Foundation.

Lang, P. (1985) 'Schooling and Welfare: Taking Account of the views and feelings of pupils' in Ribbins, P. (ed) *Schooling and Welfare.* Basingstoke: Falmer.

Lang, P. (1988) 'Primary and middle school teachers' attitudes to pastoral provision and personal and social education' in Lang, P. (ed) *Thinking...About Personal and Social Education in the Primary School.* Oxford: Basil Blackwell.

Lang, P. (1988) *Thinking...About Personal and Social Education in the Primary School.* Oxford: Basil Blackwell.

Lawrence, D. (1971) 'The effects of counselling on retarded readers'. *Educational Research* 13 (2).

Lawrence, D. (1972) 'Counselling of retarded readers by non-professionals'. *Educational Research* 15 (1).

Lewis, A. (1991) *Primary Special Needs and the National Curriculum.* London: Routledge.

Meadows, S. and Cashden, A. (1988) *Helping Children Learn.* London: David Fulton.

Measor, L. and Woods, P. (1984) *Changing Schools.* Milton Keynes: Open University Press.

Murgatroyd, S. (ed) (1980) *Helping the Troubled Child: Interprofessional Case Studies.* London: Harper and Row.

Sokolov, I. and Hutton, D. (1988) *The Parents Book.* Wellingborough: Thorsons.

Stainton-Rogers, R. (1989) 'The Social Construction of Childhood' in Stainton-Rogers, W., Hevey, D. and Ash, E. (eds) *Child Abuse and Neglect: facing the challenge.* London: Batsford.

Stott, D.H. (1978) *Helping Children with Learning Difficulties.* London: Ward Lock Educational.

Wiltshire County Council (1991) *All-Round Success: practical ideas to enhance the self-esteem of all children in the primary classroom.*

CHAPTER 3

Counselling in a Secondary Setting – Developing Policy and Practice

Colleen McLaughlin

In this chapter Colleen McLaughlin looks at current issues related to counselling and guidance in secondary schools and colleges. She looks at different aspects of counselling and highlights three areas of work – the educative, the reflective, and the welfare elements. She argues that schools need to develop clear policy in this area of work and she develops a framework for policy development.

Introduction

In this chapter I propose to explore how secondary schools and colleges can work towards the development of a policy on counselling and guidance. There has been much very useful writing about the nature of, and the purpose of, counselling in schools. The writing largely focuses on how schools can effectively use the one-to-one model of counselling and the issues this raises for teachers and managers. Much of this writing was in the 1970s and early 1980s and reflects the thinking of the time and the development of counselling practice then. It focuses on the problem-solving and developmental nature of counselling and often assumes the existence of a role similar to that of a school counsellor – a role which rarely exists now in secondary schools and 16–19 colleges. In the 1990s there is a need to look more closely at the nature of counselling in an applied setting and at the educative, as well as the problem-solving, role it can play. HMI's survey of guidance (DES, 1990) highlighted the issue of the lack of policy development in this area and stated that institutions rarely had policy statements on guidance.

In exploring the development of policy I shall examine the part counselling and guidance have to play in schools; the issues raised about counselling and guidance in these settings; and set out a framework for developing and managing this work.

Background to counselling in secondary schools

As already suggested, if one looks at the development of counselling in secondary settings the model is largely one based on problem-solving work with individuals or groups. This reflects the developments in training and thinking. In the 1970s the predominance of the Rogerian or 'client-centred' model can be seen. There were counselling training courses for those wishing to become counsellors in schools, where counsellors did exist. Their existence was not always unproblematic (cf. Richardson, 1974) but many schools employed them. In the early 1980s many factors impinged to change the situation. First, there were cuts in education spending and counsellors came to be seen as a luxury; in many local authorities counselling posts were the first to be cut. Second, there was an increase in the emphasis on counselling skills for *all* teachers, influenced by the work of people such as Egan (1986). This was in contrast to the emphasis on the Rogerian model. Third, there was an increasing interest and debate on the use of counselling in applied settings, that is in settings where counselling was not the primary task of those engaging in it (cf. Brigid Proctor's chapter in this volume). Fourth, there was an increase in the development of programmes of work for students which aimed to give the concepts of counselling and guidance to the students. This was once termed psychological education in the USA. These programmes were often called guidance programmes or personal and social education courses and they developed the teacher's role from a reactive to an educative one.

Since then, there have been further developments in the area of counselling. Many initiatives have drawn on counselling skills, such as records of achievement and teacher appraisal. In such initiatives the skills are very similar but their intentions are different, for largely the skills are being drawn on to enhance communication. Other developments have drawn on counselling psychology and theory. For example, there has also been much work in the pastoral field on bullying and child abuse. The initiatives in this area emphasise the importance of respect for students and their feelings. These developments have been accompanied by an increasing awareness of what the emotional world of schooling looks and feels like to students. An example is the acknowledgement that behaviours such as teasing and bullying have an adverse effect on students' mental health and development.

So there is much work occurring in the area of guidance and counselling. However, the development of different models and the accumulation of new functions, e.g. the educative added to the problem-solving, has led to much confusion or lack of time to sort out how these different elements work together and what the differences between the contributions are. The HMI (DES, 1990) survey reflects this position. The survey concentrated on students aged 13 to 19 in 26 maintained secondary schools and sixth form colleges: the schools included the full range of size, setting and location. The survey showed that 'schools and colleges had a variety of approaches to guidance'. The report acknowledged that a range of activities contributes to appropriate provision in this area and that many schools are contributing well. The best responses were characterised by:

- clarity and precision;
- evidence of a coherent underlying policy;
- an integrated approach (bringing together personal and social education, pastoral work, the role of subject teaching, relationships with parents and outside agencies, ethos, teaching and learning styles);
- a recognition that the quality of guidance was influenced by the school–student–home partnership;
- a relating of guidance provision to students' needs and perceptions;
- evidence of a link between intentions and practice.

The conceptions of guidance were wide ranging and not necessarily mutually exclusive. They included:

- non-directive guidance in response to students seeking help;
- guidance that sought to direct students along a particular path;
- crisis and problem-solving guidance;
- guidance built into the curriculum;
- guidance provided to meet institutional perceptions that govern-

ment and employers thought guidance was important in providing efficient matching of talents and motivation to jobs;
● guidance perceived as a specialist function of those with relevant training.

These conceptions covered 'both formal and informal arrangements and many existed, quite reasonably, side by side in the same institution; however, there were cases where there was some inconsistency in the various practices adopted. This could usually be related to the absence of explicit aims, of clearly identified elements of guidance provision and of evaluation of outcomes.' (HMI, 1990) All these issues need to be considered in the development of a clear policy and integrated practice.

Aims of counselling in secondary schools and colleges

Section 1 of the Education Reform Act states that schools have a statutory responsibility to develop a curriculum which 'promotes the spiritual, moral, cultural, mental and physical development of students at the school and of society; and prepares such students for the opportunities, responsibilities and experiences of adult life.' Guidance plays a part in helping schools to fulfil this commitment. The aim is to contribute as fully and as positively as possible to the mental health of the students in the school community and to do this in different ways: through the curriculum, through the community of the school and through one-to-one and group work.

Counselling and guidance have a developmental function as well as a reactive one. Early in the development of counselling in schools the task was seen as involving teachers in working one-to-one with students and viewed as developmental in nature. The objectives of counselling were related to:

● fostering self acceptance in students and not changing or remediating personality;
● developing control from within or fostering an internal locus of control;
● helping students to learn strategies and coping skills for situations which were difficult or important in terms of their impact on future life. (Hamblin, 1974)

These aims have not changed but there was a realisation that in a school context the work could play a more educative role. Marland (1980) summed it up when he talked of the art of giving individual guidance without having to give it individually. It is interesting to see how many of the key figures in counselling progressed to writing in the widest sense about schools and their impact on individuals (Glasser, 1969; Rogers, 1983).

Schools have a responsibility to develop students personally and socially, so there is an *educative* function. However, personal and social development do not take place in isolation. Our personal development and sense of identity are learned in our interactions with others. We learn who we are in the context of a community and those in it. Therefore, there is also the responsibility to explore the impact of the school or college on the personal and social development of the students there. This *reflective* or evaluative function involves exploring the possible impact of and contribution to personal and social development of practices in the classroom and other aspects of the school community. This generally incorporates interactions between teachers and students as well as between students and students. It also includes wider issues of teaching and learning styles, classroom and school climate. In addition, there is the *welfare* function: the responsibility to plan for and react to issues which impact on students' welfare and development. This is the area where counselling has traditionally been seen to play a part. It is helpful to distinguish these different aims but there is also the need to co-ordinate them and see the links between them. HMI (DES, 1990) states, 'Generally speaking the greatest strength of the guidance lay in its pervasiveness.' It is important to see the task as one of identifying the different strands of the web rather than developing separate and unconnected practices. 'Guidance in the classroom was most successful where teaching and learning were of good quality.' (*ibid.*) If this is to be the case then co-ordination and management of provision become very important, as does exploring the reality of the school's or college's provision.

The educative element

The educative element includes guidance in the curriculum as well as the wider field of affective education or education for the emotions. In terms of guidance in the curriculum, the framework of personal, vocational and educational guidance is now a well accepted one. It is often hard to distinguish between them. The curriculum is related to the different needs and ages of students. It should also reflect the particular needs of students in relation to their community and context. Much of this element can be planned in advance using frameworks which have been tried and tested – for example, the framework for vocational guidance of developing decision making, transition learning, opportunity awareness and self-awareness. It includes giving students the personal and social skills without which they may require problem based counselling – for example, helping students acquire the skills of listening and responding appropriately to others, or developing the ability to express feelings and opinions. It also contains elements which are in response to guidance needs perceived as arising from particular themes in groups or individuals. This may include working on topics such as friendship or negotiation, as well as the experience and development of the ability to work in a group. Many of the issues which were responded to by teachers on an individual basis, such as bullying, are now being acknowledged as issues which need to be dealt with in an educative way through the curriculum. Responding to these issues on an ad hoc basis is no longer adequate.

We also know that the time of vulnerability for many students is at periods of transition (Hamblin, 1974; DES, 1990). Hamblin (*ibid.*) called these 'critical incidents'. They are critical because they are occasions when students can affiliate to the school or become alienated. At these times, such as entry to school, transfer to new courses or transfer to new institutions, students need support and this support needs to be of an organised form and have a curricular element. The HMI survey (DES, 1990) noted that, 'All institutions understood the necessity of offering substantial guidance at these stages and most provided guidance that was overall sound in many respects.' However, they identified guidance in Year 9 as often inadequate and they emphasise the importance of guidance at 13 +. In providing effective guidance there is a need to plan a programme which is coherent and not merely a collection of one-off events. Guidance is most effective when it is continual and cumulative (Wall, 1977; McPhail, 1972). The same themes will recur and yet will differ according to the age and stage the students have reached.

So far I have commented on what could be called the 'content' of guidance curriculum. However, there are other elements of the educative function. These are to do with the way in which such guidance programmes or elements are delivered, as well as the context and processes of the learning. Guidance teaching requires an awareness of the appropriate methods in this field, for example the ability to help students think for themselves or the ability to work with groups rather than individuals. HMI (DES, 1990) identified three areas of weakness here. First, 'not all teachers involved being at ease with various aspects of content and approaches'; second, 'over-reliance on commercially reproduced schemes and duplicated work-sheets so that students were not encouraged to think for themselves'; and third, 'failure to achieve appropriate balance between content and related personal, vocational and educational issues'. Many teachers still do not have the opportunities to develop a range of teaching styles. It is many years now since Bolam and Medlock (1985) charted the difficulties and complexities involved in developing the skills of working with groups and other such teaching techniques. The recent debates on teaching and learning in schools reflect many of the unhelpful polarisations that were present in education many years ago. Teachers need to be able to use a repertoire of teaching styles and to be able to choose consciously from them, being aware of the impact that each one has. There is considerable evidence to show that techniques such as co-operative learning do impact on students' personal and social development (Slavin, 1983; Johnson and Johnson, 1982). This is not to argue for this as the sole method of learning but rather for its consideration and inclusion in the range of learning experiences which students have.

The educative element also has implications for the context of the classroom. The creation of an appropriate classroom climate and the establishment of procedures is as important as the content and teaching format. There are many complex issues here. In a recent study of girls' development Mikel Brown and Gilligan (1982) show that during adolescence girls lose the ability to express their real feelings and opinions. They describe this as a loss of voice. They argue that girls do this to avoid endangering relationships and that it has long term consequences for the development of women. As a result they argue for the need to encourage adolescent girls to express difference and disagreement. This would suggest that procedures in the classroom, such as the negotiation of ground rules and rules for constructive controversy, are important. Certain programmes of work are exemplars of this. *Skills for Adolescence* (Tacade, 1986) includes procedures and rules regarding how students listen to one another or demonstrate respect. The Elton Report (DES, 1989) on discipline in schools has also emphasised the importance of students' negotiating rules and procedures, as well as having opportunities for the expression of opinion. The classroom context, the procedures and the nature of the interactions all impact on student self-image and self-esteem. These are important elements in motivation as well as important elements in the school's contribution to personal and social development.

Other processes, such as the development of self assessment and the formation of action plans, facilitate the personal development of students. In the one-to-one dialogues with students, teachers are required to use skills drawn from counselling. It is important to distinguish between drawing on counselling skills to make communication effective and conducting a counselling interview. The ethical constraints, the boundaries of the talk and the student's choosing of that dialogue are all important differences between the two activities. However, both are skilled activities and HMI (DES, 1990) comment that many teachers were not adequately trained for the records of achievement dialogues and, as a result, the work was often superficial.

In summary it can be said that in terms of policy formation at this level the tasks are to co-ordinate the curriculum content and delivery; to examine the context of the learning; and to ensure that teacher development in these areas is addressed.

The reflective element

I stated earlier that the reflective function was related to an exploration of the impact of the school on the personal and social development, as well as the mental health, of the students. This is to argue that the role of counselling is to promote healthy institutions as well as healthy individuals. Recent research has shown that schools can have a substantial impact on children's psychological development both in the present and in the future. Rutter (1991) sums up much of his own and others' research in these words:

> It is no easy matter to create a happy, effective school and there are a variety of influences outside the control of the schools. Nevertheless, schooling does matter greatly. Moreover, the benefits can be surprisingly long-lasting. This is *not* because school experiences have a permanent effect on a child's psychological brain structure, but rather because experiences at one point in a child's life tend to influence what happens afterwards in a complicated set of indirect chain reactions. It is crucial to appreciate that these long-term benefits rely on *both* effects on cognitive performance (in terms of learning specific skills, improved task orientation and better persistence) *and* effects of self-esteem and self-efficacy (with respect to better attitudes to learning, raised parental expectations and more positive teacher responses because children are more rewarding to teach). (p. 9)

Recently we have seen a development in approach to many issues which reflects this position of developing schools as healthy environments personally, socially and academically. An example is the approach advocated in the Elton Report (DES, 1989). Previously the disciplinary role of the school was largely to do with the reaction to incidents of bad behaviour, although there were of course attempts to foster positive behaviour. The Elton Report argued for the promotion of positive behaviour. It was a much more proactive and wide ranging approach, one which acknowledged the role of *all* in the school community and which shifted the emphasis to a concentration on developing positive behaviour rather than focusing on problem behaviours. Similarly, in the area of counselling and guidance I would want to argue for a more proactive and wide ranging approach. This should reflect the promotion of positive strategies to developing mental health rather than a focus on reacting to problem situations, although I am not arguing for the exclusion of the latter. It is an argument for reflection on aspects of school or college life which may not come under the heading of the formal curriculum.

This reflection is the work of pastoral care. Just as Mikel Brown and Gilligan's work (1992) shows how interactions in the classroom can impact on girls' development, so we are becoming aware of the impact of other aspects of school life on the learning and development of students. The nature of students' interactions with other students is an example. Recent initiatives in child abuse and bullying, allied to an emphasis on children's rights, have alerted us to what the experience of young people is. The voices of young people are being heard more clearly and the nature of their experience is being acknowledged more fully. In reaction to this teachers and others (Besag, 1989) have argued for intervention by teachers and the co-ordination of approaches in the curriculum as well as in response to incidents. The task here then is to explore the school as a community and examine its impact on students and teachers. It will involve teachers in actively inviting students to give feedback on the functioning and health of the school and its practices. This may engage teachers in debates about teacher–student interactions and the values underpinning them – a difficult and controversial area for many to engage in.

The health of the institution also involves exploration of areas which are the responsibility of management. The health of the adults is also up for scrutiny here. Recently there has been much debate about the workplace and teachers. Barth (1991) has focused on the nature of adult interaction in school and the emotional health of schools. He has argued that there is much to be done to improve the nature of schools as healthy places for the adults in them and that there is a need to take this issue more seriously. Surveys on teacher stress and discussions in this field have led many to argue for counselling for staff. It may be the case that there is a need for such services but there is also a danger here that adoption of the one-to-one problem-solving model will be to the exclusion of debating wider issues such as support for staff in their professional roles and work (cf. Lodge, McLaughlin and Best, 1992).

The welfare element

The welfare aspect of counselling and guidance is the area most focused on and developed in writing about counselling in school settings. Hamblin (1974) described the school's role as that of being 'a guidance community'. The objectives in this area are:

- to aid students in decision making and problem-solving;
- to support students in a constructive manner at times of difficulty;
- to monitor and detect students who are at risk or under pressure;
- to react in appropriate fashion;
- to co-ordinate work within and outside the school.

The area will include a range of activities mentioned earlier: for example, counselling when it is sought by students; more focused guidance activities such as that involved in decision making of a predictable kind; counselling to react to crisis, problems and transitions; and more specialist counselling. It will also involve liaising with outside agencies and parents.

These activities require many and different skills and abilities. They also require practitioners to be able to distinguish between these different activities. The work of John Heron (1990) is helpful here. Heron argues that there are six possible types of intervention between practitioner and client. By an intervention he means 'an identifiable piece of verbal and/or nonverbal behaviour that is part of the practitioner's service to the client'. (p. 3) The six categories are subdivided into two main types – authoritative and facilitative. These are shown in Figure 3.1.

The first three categories are called authoritative because they are rather more hierarchical – the practitioner is taking responsibility for

AUTHORITATIVE

1. Prescriptive
   A prescriptive intervention seeks to direct the behaviour of the client, usually behaviour that is outside the practitioner–client relationship.
2. Informative
   An informative intervention seeks to impart knowledge, information, meaning to the client.
3. Confronting
   A confronting intervention seeks to raise the client's consciousness about some limiting attitude or behaviour of which they are relatively unaware.

FACILITATIVE

4. Cathartic
   A cathartic intervention seeks to enable the client to discharge, to abreact painful emotion, primarily grief, fear and anger.
5. Catalytic
   A catalytic intervention seeks to elicit self-discovery, self-directed living, learning and problem-solving in the client.
6. Supportive
   A supportive intervention seeks to affirm the worth and value of the client's person, qualities, attitudes or actions.

Figure 3.1   The six categories of counselling intervention (Heron, 1990)

and on behalf of the client. The second three are called facilitative because they are rather less hierarchical – the practitioner is seeking to enable clients to become more autonomous and take more responsibility for themselves. Heron (*ibid*.) comments that 'Traditional education and training have rather overdone authoritative sorts of interventions and have often omitted the facilitative sorts altogether.' (p. 6) Heron argues that the skilled practitioner is someone who is equally proficient in a wide range of interventions in each of the categories; can move elegantly, flexibly and cleanly from one intervention to another as the situation and purposes require; is aware at any given time of what intervention he/she is using; knows when to lead the client and when to follow; and has a creative balance between power over the client, power shared with the client and the facilitation of power within the client.

This is helpful to our work in schools and as a framework for teacher development. It can also highlight some of the problems of work in schools. I have detected some confusion about the role and type of interventions that are described in schools as counselling interventions. For example, wanting to change someone's behaviour because it causes problems for the school or is seen as unacceptable by a particular teacher is not necessarily a prescriptive counselling intervention. Hamblin (1974) has described vividly the misuses of counselling in schools. He has argued that counselling is not about personality change; it is not solely for those perceived as 'deviant' and 'disadvantaged'; it is not an opportunity to exercise subtle control or manipulation; nor is it probing into the student's private world. HMI (DES, 1990) comments on the lack of clarity between discipline and counselling, saying that 'staff and students often perceived a clash between guidance and the need to enforce discipline'.

There is a need to establish some principles which help to distinguish counselling from other activities in schools. The first is that counselling is something which the student must be aware is occurring and which must in some way be chosen. I am not implying that this requires that counselling can only be student initiated but rather that it should be invitational in nature. For example, the teacher might say, 'Would you like to talk about this?' There is an assumption inbuilt into counselling that the student can change – it is an essentially optimistic, but not unrealistic, activity. The student's needs are paramount in counselling rather than the needs of the school or the teacher, although the student may need to know the views and perceptions of others. The counselling should aim generally to empower the student and to develop a sense of control and autonomy. The relationship in which the counselling takes place should be:

- respectful (including an acknowledgement of and respect for the views and experiences of others different from ourselves);
- genuine on the part of the teacher;
- and aim to demonstrate empathy.

In addition, the counselling should include the full range of counselling interventions and be practically helpful to the student. Heron (1990) argues that a valid intervention is one which is 'appropriate to the client's current state and stage of development and to the developing practitioner–client interaction. To say that it is appropriate is to say that: (a) it is in the right category; (b) it is the right sort of intervention within the category; (c) its content and use of language is fitting; (d) it is delivered in the right manner; and (e) it is delivered with good timing.'

Some of the issues being debated here are to do with a specialist level of work and it would be helpful to distinguish between the different levels of work in schools and colleges. Hamblin (1974) distinguished three levels of work in schools:

48

(1) *The immediate level*

This level of work is for all teachers in the school and involves the use of first level counselling skills and an awareness of what counselling is. Counselling skills will be used to facilitate good communication as well as to acknowledge the emotional dimension of learning and living. Reasonable demands would be made on students and teachers. Teachers would be able to work in the emotional domain, adapting to individuals and groups in the light of what is known, and providing reinforcement and support. Teachers would also be involved in detecting signs of stress and tension in students and communicating this to others if that is appropriate. Hamblin (*ibid.*) calls this an exploratory and screening function. This level of work may involve working with teachers and other professionals.

(2) *The intermediate level*

Here Hamblin argues that the school or college is concerned to provide continuity of care, concern and relationships. It is to do with the co-ordination of efforts and resources, including those outside of the school setting. It is also to do with the establishment and operation of systems which act as early warnings of students who may need counselling and guidance. This means that systems of communication need to be established, monitored and reviewed. The HMI survey (DES, 1990) commented on aspects of provision at this level. It highlighted the importance of good record keeping, 'including recording interviews held with students, by whom, when, for what purpose and with what result'. Part of the co-ordination of resources includes knowing what training and expertise exists amongst the staff. The HMI survey comments that 'Successful practice involved adults who had special training, qualities or experience (or more often all three) and included trained counsellors, chaplains, matrons and nurses as well as some individual pastoral staff. However, counselling was often ad hoc, dealt with problems which had simmered unattended for too long, and was undertaken by teachers who lacked training in counselling skills. Several teachers who had received counselling training were not always in positions where such skills could be put to good use.' (p. 38)

(3) *The specialist level*

This level demands training for the task and this expertise may reside within the school or outside of it. It also involves the identification of students who may require this level of help. It may involve specialists in the running of groups as well as working with individuals.

In the formation of policy the levels of work and the training needs of the teachers need to be determined. The provision needs to be evaluated and managed. There are many professional and practical issues which need to be debated alongside matters of who does what and how.

Ethical and professional issues

Part of the ethical requirements of schools is to monitor and evaluate the nature of the provision. In the HMI survey (DES, 1990) it was clear that this was not a common activity. Only two institutions 'had a systematic approach to evaluating the planning, processes and outcomes of the personal, educational and vocational guidance offered to students'. There is also a responsibility to ensure that staff are equipped to provide adequate counselling and guidance and this involves looking at the training and development needs of the staff.

Confidentiality is another ethical matter which the school or college needs to debate. There is rarely a clear statement on this issue and students often receive very mixed messages on this. The school setting is a complex one to work in regarding this issue. There is a desire to protect student privacy and at the same time there are legal requirements which prevent the promising of total confidentiality to students in certain areas of work, for example child abuse. What is important is that both staff and students are aware of the limits of confidentiality in various settings and types of interview, as well as being aware of what happens to information shared with teachers and other professionals.

Staff working in this area also need professional support and a forum to debate some of the difficult professional and moral decisions which may occur. HMI (*ibid.*) found examples 'of networks or groups of teachers coming together to plan specific initiatives or to review aspects of a school's or college's work'.

Management issues

Apart from managing the development of policy on ethical and professional support there are many other management issues. The provision of private spaces for counselling and guidance work is important. HMI (DES, 1990) comment that 'effective guidance was promoted where the physical environment was such as to encourage good relationships and a positive ethos, and where special accommodation for a range of guidance activities was readily available and of a good standard'. The allocation of time is also important. HMI (*ibid.*) noted big variations between institutions. They concluded, 'Institutions may like to consider reviewing the time allocated for guidance, on the basis of a closer identification of need.'

HMI (*ibid.*) found that 'responsibilities for planning the use of guidance resources were usually too widely dispersed to allow for effective management'. The issue of managing staffing, training and development of staff, and co-ordinating the communication between them, is central to the management task. I have identified many of the management issues in the course of this chapter and they can be summarised as:

- a need to clarify the purposes of counselling and guidance, acknowledging the different purposes and different levels of work;
- a need to evaluate that provision, including the student voice in that process;
- a need to draw up and communicate policy in this area.

HMI (*ibid.*) found that, 'Generally speaking the greatest **strength** of the guidance seen lay in its pervasiveness... There were, however, **weaknesses** in the provision of guidance. It was seldom co-ordinated and there were rarely policies relevant to guidance... finally, more attention needed to be given to analysing the outcomes of guidance, and relating findings to planning of provision... If schools and colleges are to offer guidance of good quality they need to develop approaches which, in the light of their circumstances, achieve and maintain a proper balance between meeting the needs of the individual and of society; and between reacting to problems and taking the initiative.' (pp. 79–81)

References

Barth, R. (1991) *Improving Schools From Within*. Oxford: Jossey-Bass.

Besag, V. (1989) *Bullies and Victims in Schools*. Buckingham: Open University Press.

Bolam and Medlock (1985) *The Evaluation of Active Tutorial Work*. Oxford: Basil Blackwell.

DES (1989) *Discipline in Schools*. The Elton Report. London: HMSO.

DES (1990) *HMI Survey of Guidance 13–19 in Schools and Sixth Form Colleges*. London: DES.

Egan, G. (1986) Third edition. *The Skilled Helper*. Monterey: Brooks Cole.

Glasser (1969) *Schools without Failure*. New York: Harper and Row.

Hamblin, D. (1974) *The Teacher and Counselling*. Oxford: Blackwell.

Heron, J. (1990) *Helping the Client*. London: Sage Publications.

Johnson, D. and Johnson, F. (1982) Second edition. *Joining Together – Group Theory and Group Skills*. London: Prentice Hall.

Lodge, C., McLaughlin, C. and Best, R. (1992) 'Organizing pastoral support for teachers: some comments and a model' in *Pastoral Care in Education* Vol. 10, no. 2 pp. 7–12.

Marland, M. (1980) 'The Pastoral Curriculum' in Best, R. (1980) *Perspectives on Pastoral Care*. London: Heinemann.

McPhail, P. (1972) *Moral Education in the Secondary School*. London: Longman.

Mikel Brown, L. and Gilligan, C. (1992) *Meeting at the Crossroads – Women's Psychology and Girls' Development*. London: Harvard University Press.

Richardson, E. (1974) *The Teacher, the School and the Task of Management*. London: Heinemann.

Rogers, C. (1983) *Freedom to Learn for the Eighties*. Ohio: Charles Merrill.

Rutter, M. (1991) 'Pathways from childhood to adult life: the role of schooling' in *Pastoral Care in Education* Vol. 9, no. 3 pp. 3–10.

Slavin, R. E. (1983) *Co-operative Learning*. London: Longman.

Tacade (1986) *Skills for Adolescence*. Manchester: Tacade.

Wall, W. D. (1977) *Constructive Education for Adolescents*. London: Unesco.

CHAPTER 4

Counselling in Special Education

Keith Bovair

*The skills of counselling needed by teachers in the area of special
education are no different from those identified throughout this
book. What is different is the scale of special need and the
ramifications for the pupil, the parent or guardian, the teacher and
other individuals who offer support. This chapter focuses on pupils
and their parents, discussing their needs and the first step of
support given by an educator – listening – as promoted in the
counselling model.*

The individual

In any pupil's education, there are three main transition periods:
entering primary school, entering secondary school and entering
work or further education and training. Each one of these periods
relies on the individual to develop adaptive skills: developing new
relationships with adults and peers, conforming, acquiring an
expanded range of social relations, organising time and study skills,
becoming responsible and independent (Male and Thompson, 1985).

We need to remember that pupils start out as omnipotent
individuals who, in a normal babyhood, when they cry get fed, get
changed, get held. Later, as children, they are expected to conform at
home, at playgroup or nursery, and throughout their primary,
secondary and further education – at the end of which time they are

supposed to re-establish their individuality within the bounds of society. These transitions in childhood and adolescence are affected by the nature of the physical and emotional development of each pupil, who, at times, will be in need of support and guidance. When their development is compounded by a special need, the implications or ramifications can deeply affect not only the individual, but also a wider audience – the family, the teachers and other individuals who offer support. All can be presented with the reality of the disability; physical restrictions, the requirements for physiotherapy, speech therapy, etc., classroom organisation, access to learning, questions of future independence, and so on. These, with good practice, are not insurmountable and can be supported within a healthy, supportive school atmosphere.

Lowe (1988) states that the process of counselling and problem solving within an educational setting is an effective response to special educational needs. It can help students/pupils deal with crisis or, being preventative in nature, can provide 'a means of anticipating problems, exploring them, considering the options open to students with them and thereby increasing the probability that the students will be able to deal adequately rather than inadequately with the situation when it arises'. This response is key to ensuring that the transitions all pupils go through are met as effectively as possible. A point to remember is:

> Children with special educational needs have the same basic emotional needs as other children but they may require additional support to meet these needs. (Male and Thompson, 1985)

Additional counselling support for special needs children will vary depending on the severity of their disability and their ability to manage the transitions that they go through in their educational life. The counselling skills needed by educators working with pupils with special needs are no different from those identified throughout this book. The effectiveness of counselling to support these transitions is dependent on the resources available in each school. Encouragement for constructive models of support has been put forward for quite some time in the field of education in Great Britain. Unfortunately, as Hamblin (1974) describes, counselling has often been undermined by the following scenario:

> 'Counselling is a necessity, but counsellors are not.' This statement, made by experienced teachers, indicates that as yet there is insufficient knowledge of the specialized role, functions and techniques of the

trained school counsellor. Why do these teachers accept the activity, yet reject the role? It is possible to understand what happens through this simple illustration. As a teacher begins to read about counselling or explore it some way, he becomes aware of a feeling of familiarity. This crystallizes into a belief, 'I've been here before!' They are then in the position of the man in Moliere's play who suddenly discovered he had been speaking prose for years. The familiarity sprang from the fact that both counselling and teaching are deeply concerned with interpersonal relationships. Delight at the revelation that one has oneself already been counselling hides a vital point which seems to have escaped the man who spoke prose. Surely, once he had made the discovery, the sensible thing would have been to train himself to speak better prose.

Dialogue in staff rooms would often negate any progression in the development of interpersonal skills and the establishment of the counselling role to meet the personal and emotional needs of a pupil. A strong view, often heard, is, 'I am here to teach, not baby-sit or molly-coddle, the pupil.' Currently, this may have been seriously enhanced by the rapid changes in education with greater demand on academic performance, not only by the pupil, but also by the school's expected results in examinations (teaching to the test). This leaves little time to attend to the personal needs of the pupil.

How does such a view affect pupils with special educational needs? If they have learning difficulties which surface as reactive behaviour, it can lead to an 'accelerated' shifting of responsibility from the teacher in the ordinary setting to that of the special educator and the specialist setting. Unfortunately, what is occuring in this process is the marginalisation of individual pupils and their families. It undermines both the self worth of the pupil and the role that the parent has in this dynamic, implanting a sense of failure and/or a sense of loss in both (Bovair, 1992). There is also an assumption that the educators in these settings are trained in interpersonal skills and are able 'to speak better prose'. This is an assumption, not a fact.

Relationships with the pupil are naturally important. The skills in helping to establish them and in maintaining them apply to all who work with children and young people. An often neglected relationship is the one with the parents. This requires an understanding of their circumstances/situation, which, sometimes, is not attended to in the teacher–parent relationship. This, in my estimation, is the key to the pupil's self-growth.

Parents: dealing with a sense of loss and grief

Parents whose children have severe learning difficulties or whose special educational needs are visible, as with the physically disabled, the blind, often have a multi-professional and/or voluntary network to support both the child and the family. There is a focus for the parent in the organisations at hand, such as the National Association of Mental Health (MIND), the Spastics Society, the Royal Society for Mentally Handicapped Children and Adults (MENCAP), the National Autistic Society, which are available to disseminate information and support parents. There are also educational settings such as playgroups, pre-school special provision (Carpenter, 1990) and specialist settings/schools. The medical profession itself has a system of counselling pre-natal and family. An example of this support is in the following case study taken from Stratford (1989, pp. 105–106).

> Jane was born after a normal pregnancy and labour. A few hours after the birth, the doctor confirmed that she was a child with Down's Syndrome. She took her first steps at 18 months and said her first words at 2 years. At 2½ she started to attend an 'opportunity playgroup' and at 3½ was enroled at a day school for children with severe learning difficulties. Here she was placed on an intensive language remediation programme, so that by the age of 7 not only was she talking fluently but she also had a reading age of 6 years. She could count up to twenty and could add numbers up to ten, using counters. The psychologist and the medical officer consulted with both the headmistress and with her parents, and it was decided that Jane should be given the opportunity of integration into the ordinary school. She was therefore found a place in a slow learner unit for children with moderate learning difficulties attached to such a school. Again, Jane progressed well. She required considerable help and support from her teacher but made steady if slow educational progress. She became much more socially confident than perhaps she would have been had she remained in special school. At the age of 11, Jane had a reading age of 8 years and was transferred to another slow learner unit attached to her local secondary school. Towards the end of her school career she began to experience some difficulties. Though she could cope with a limited range of social activities, her peers had begun to outstrip her socially and educationally and to have vocational aims which she would not be able to realize. However, in her last year in school she was able to attend a bridging course arranged for mentally handicapped children at a College of Further Education. The career guidance officer decided that she would fit in

well in a sheltered workshop, and a place was found for her. Jane now lives at home and attends the adult training centre where she is considered to be one of the more socially competent members of her group.

This case study illustrates a constructive development in the life of a child with Down's Syndrome. In the background there appears to be a healthy support network, for it was remarked that the parents were 'proud and satisfied with her progress'. Unfortunately there is a large population of parents who do feel marginalised and unsupported (Bell, 1987). They are parents of children with moderate learning difficulties – the largest population of children identified as having special educational needs. When these parents do seek help on behalf of their children, they are sometimes discounted as over anxious, protective and awkward. But, as one parent describes, it is necessary to be assertive and sometimes manipulate the system.

> I always – sort of – pretend she has severe learning difficulties. It's better that way, you get special help and things. (Russell, 1992, Appendix 7, p. xxix)

Parents of children with moderate learning or physical difficulties sometimes suffer a greater sense of loss when these difficulties present themselves when a child is older. It is because comparisons can be made between how they were and how they are now.

> 'It seems twice as heartbreaking,' she said, 'when I remember how he used to climb everything in sight.' Behmer (1976, p. 8)

Le Poidevin (1983), on bereavement, and Cameron (1984) identify that the process of grief in the loss of life is comparable to the sense of loss when a child is identified as having a special need. Cameron is a parent of a child with special needs. She has paralleled her experiences with her son, Tom, and Le Poidevin's work. Some of the similarities are:

- shock;
- incomprehension of loss;
- rejection;
- continuous questioning;
- swings of moods (elation/depression);
- sense of social isolation;
- a need to justify/explain;
- desire to be accepted;

- fear of future;
- nightmares/fantasies;
- unable to organise;
- energetic/apathetic.

As Behmer (1976) states, 'Grief for the perfect child one has lost is a genuine part of the parents' feelings.'

How many parents do we encounter in our day to day work in special education, who have similar experiences and who are going through a process of a sense of loss – loss of the normal child? How many feel powerless in dealing with the reality of recognising their child has a special need? What counselling skills are necessary for the teacher to support these individuals? How can the teacher handle these feelings? What can they do when presented with a situation as illustrated in the following case?

> A young mother with a child, age 7, who has moderate learning difficulties and is attending a primary school, is, after years of attempting to find help, informed that the school can no longer assist the child and that the child would have to attend special school. She makes an appointment and visits the prescribed school. The mother in interview identifies her feelings of failure because her child may be attending a special school. She feels guilty she hadn't succeeded in getting earlier support for her child. She feels guilty and powerless (although she needn't be) in the final judgement for placement and she senses the professional pressure for her 'not to be awkward' and go along with the recommendations 'for the sake of her child'.

In such a case, the headteacher of the school could be patronising with a 'there, there' approach, asserting his or her professionalism/expertise in such matters, possibly compounding the mother's feelings of inadequacy as a parent. Or he/she could listen, drawing out the parent's concerns and identifying an agenda for action, which would allow the parent to properly weigh up an effective way forward in ensuring that the most appropriate education is provided for her child.

Here, the headteacher chose the latter approach, identifying the parents' rights and possible alternatives for educational support besides the special school placement. He also reassured the mother that if she felt special schooling was correct, then the school, in partnership with her, would do all in its power to compensate for the perceived loss in her child's education. The key point is that she was empowered to make a personal decision.

Skills: the first steps

The first skills required of any teacher dealing with parents are:

- an empathy for their situation;
- an understanding of the impact of grief on a family's life;
- an understanding of the complexity in family dynamics;
- an ability to listen.

To understand the impact of grief we can return to Cameron's emotions felt during the loss of the 'normal' child. We soon can recognise stages at which we may have encountered parents when we have been discussing their child's needs. Without this knowledge we may have perceived the parent as awkward and obstructive, defensive and over sensitive; but on closer study we can quickly identify the behaviour as a process in dealing with a harsh reality; a process which needs support. Teachers can be the first step; they can be a 'travelling companion', rather than the 'expert', and in that companionship the educator learns to 'speak better prose'.

In 'speaking better prose', for all educators the non-directive approach put forward by Carl Rogers (1961) is one means of constructively helping the individual. It is the most popular and frequently used approach. Two components are empathy and unconditional positive regard (valuing the individual), and a third is non-possessive warmth. Within this model, the skill of reflection and facilitating empowers individuals to take responsibility for their actions and their lives. In this framework, teachers who are not fully trained counsellors can still use this approach to enhance the quality in relationships, which is the key to resolving many situations encountered in the educational setting.

The strongest support that a teacher can offer any parent is that of listening. We all listen, but do we hear? In Figure 4.1, Mallon (1987) sets out specific listening skills.

Listening is a powerful tool as the following case study may attest.

Paul – now 14 years of age – was originally referred and placed in a special school for children with moderate learning difficulties at the age of 10 – primary transfer age. He exhibited a variety of learning difficulties – speech and language, writing and reading and the physical symptoms of a 'clumsy' child.

Paul came from a family of five – successful professional parents and a talented brother and sister. Expectations of academic success were high; the reality of Paul's limited ability brought the family to a low.

The father had disengaged from involvement with Paul. The mother

Figure 4.1   Specific listening skills © Mallon, B. (1987) *An Introduction to Counselling Skills for Special Educational Needs*. Manchester University Press.

Types	Purpose	Examples
1. Warmth, support	To help the client to feel at ease	I'd like to help . . . Are you able to tell me about your concern?
2. Clarification	To elicit complete information	Can you tell me more about it?
	To assist client to explore whole issue	Do you mean . . . ?
3. Restatement	To check our meaning is the same as the client's	From what you are saying I understand that . . .
	To show understanding	So, you've decided to . . .
4. Encouragement	To encourage the client	I realise this is difficult for you, but you're doing really well . . .
5. Reflective	To act as a mirror for the client to see what is being communicated	You feel that . . .
		It was very hard for you to accept . . .
	To help clients evaluate their feelings	You felt angry and upset when they . . .
	To show you understand the feeling behind the words	
6. Summarising	To bring together the areas discussed so far	These are the main points which have emerged . . .
	To provide a starting point for future work	As I see it, your main concern seems to be . . .

carried the responsibility of trying to ensure that he was given the education due to him. In this, she appeared abrasive, abrupt and defensive in her dealings with the school. She would challenge any report.

To compound matters, it was discovered that Paul had a degenerative muscle disease. This accelerated while he was at the special school, where staff, children and especially his family bore witness to watching a fairly mobile young person become dependent on equipment for mobility. Yet, though dependent, he was determined to be as independent as possible, taking part in school activities, even an adventure holiday, where he was captured on video abseiling.

In a review session, it was noted by the teacher that the only dialogue and correspondence between home and school about Paul had been looking at his difficulties, not his strengths – in particular, his determination to attempt things. Both parents were present and they agreed that this occurs and expressed how they felt about it. At this point the mother became very emotional and the father silent. The teacher in the review 'listened' in the true sense of the model (Figure 4.1) and a great wealth of information came forward about the family's feelings. During the course of this, the father contributed, identifying his disappointments and his feeling of isolation. He felt that if he talked with his wife about his feelings, it would only burden her further. They both spoke of their sense of loss. This was a new starting point for the parents and the school.

At future meetings, discussions about Paul's strengths (for he had many) were highlighted. The parents viewed the video and were pleased and proud of what they saw him accomplish. Open discussions about his future were shared by all. Father began to take a more active interest in his education and school life and the mother felt she was not alone; support was there from the school and the husband. This was achieved by 'listening'.

Conclusion

The value of partnership with parents in education is clearly identified in the work of Cunningham and Davis (1985). Twenty years' experience of working with children, families and guardians in the area of special education has led me to acknowledge that individual counselling is a very important aspect of this work, but the most powerful change agent for the well being of a pupil with special educational needs is not only the relationship with the pupil, but also the relationship between the school, the teacher and the family or guardian. It is tempting, as 'professionals', to be directive but as Davis (1985) points out in an example of working with children with behaviour problems and their parents:

> Given a non-directive approach, some parents would talk for hours.... They would address many other problems, issues and experiences relevant to themselves, the child and the family as a whole. More interesting, however, was that such discussions were not uncommonly associated with improvements in the child's behaviour, even when the behaviour had not been discussed or actively tackled. Again, in situations where a child's behaviour did not change as a

result of an intervention programme, parents themselves sometimes changed positively, becoming more lively, confident, happy and effective. (p. 20)

As in all relationships, the sense of being valued, empowered and listened to, having empathetic support and concern is important for growth. To paraphrase Davis (*ibid.*), the starting points in dealing with the Why's, How's, When's and Where's presented by parents are:

- identifying what the parents know and think;
- developing the most useful understanding to enable predictions as to what to do (this depends on whether parents have an effective approach already, which enables effective action);
- providing information if required (parents may lack understanding of, or misconstrue, previous information given by 'professionals/experts');
- guiding their observations, making suggestions about possible explanations, thus enabling parents to take positive actions.

Parents can then

- set explicit and realistic goals;
- decide on and prepare acceptable and useful practical methods of reaching goals;
- determine if the strategies were effective and review them for themselves.

The teacher can work in partnership with the parent in this process and be a 'listener' as Lao-Tze wrote:

It is as though he listened
and such listening as his enfolds us in a silence
in which at last we begin to hear
what we are meant to be (Rogers, 1980, p. 41).

In establishing what the parents are 'meant to be', a secure base for the pupil is established. In supporting and guiding the pupil, we then have a better chance in establishing what they feel they are 'meant to be'.

References

Behmer, M. R. (1976) Coping with our Children's Disabilities: Some Basic Principles, in *The Exceptional Parent* Vol. 6, No. 2.

Bell, B. (1987) *The Needs of Parents of Pre-School Children with Special Educational Needs in Hertfordshire.* Unpublished MEd., Hertfordshire College of Higher Education.

Bovair, K. (1992) *Children and Young Persons' Perceptions of Reasons for Placement in a Special Educational Setting for those Experiencing Emotional and Behavioural Difficulties.* Research Project funded by the Kellmer Pringle Fellowship 1991–1992, National Children's Bureau.

Cameron, J. (1984) 'A parent's view', in Dessent, T. *What is Important About Portage?* London: NFER-Nelson.

Carpenter, B. (1990) Joining Forces: Parental Participation in the Development of a Community Integrated Nursery, in *Early Child Development and Care*, Vol. 64, pp. 47–54.

Cunningham, C. and Davis, H. (1985) *Working with Parents: Framework for Collaboration.* Milton Keynes: Open University Press.

Davis, H. (1985) Counselling Parents of Children Who Have Intellectual Disabilities, in *Early Child Development and Care*, Vol. 22, pp. 19–35.

Hamblin, D. (1974) *The Teacher and Counselling.* Oxford: Basil Blackwell.

Le Poidevin, S. (1983) *Bereavement Rehabilitation Model.* Paper provided from St Christopher's Hospice, 51–53 Lawrie Park Road, London S.E. 26.

Lowe, P. (1988) *Responding to Adolescent Needs; a pastoral care approach.* London: Cassell.

Male, J. and Thompson, C. (1985) *The Educational Implications of Disability.* London: RADAR.

Mallon, B. (1987) *An Introduction to Counselling Skills for Special Educational Needs.* Manchester: Manchester University Press.

Rogers, C. (1961) *On Becoming a Person.* Boston: Houghton Mifflin.

Rogers, C. (1980) *A Way of Being.* Boston: Houghton Mifflin.

Russell, P. (1992) *The Needs of Children with Learning Difficulties and Their Families, Learning Difficulties*, a unit of the Distance Learning Course for Teachers of Children with Learning Difficulties (Severe & Moderate). School of Education, The University of Birmingham.

Stratford, B. (1989) *Down's Syndrome.* London: Penguin Books.

CHAPTER 5

Counselling Abused Children in Schools

Neil Hall

Child abuse is a major concern for all professionals working with children and young people. In this chapter, Neil Hall brings forward information which will raise awareness, recommend whole school approaches and identify skills required in counselling and supporting individuals whose lives are compounded by such events.

Introduction

Reliable data on the extent and nature of child abuse is scarce. The information which does exist is widely regarded as being a considerable under-estimate of the total number of children and adolescents who have been abused. Moreover, of those pupils who have been identified as experiencing some form of abuse, or at-risk of being abused, there is still very little known concerning the counselling services that may have been provided for them in educational settings. The situation is particularly unclear about which pupils are receiving what kind of individual or group counselling. Equally, the full extent of whole-school initiatives, or those involving parents, the wider community, or school governors is virtually uncharted. Additionally, given the very small percentage of trained counsellors who work specifically in British schools, or offer part-time/sessional services to them, and the increasing numbers of abused/at-risk children, the potential demand for counselling interventions for these children could become a significant aspect of future educational provision. There is certainly considerable scope for research and evaluation of work in this vital area.

However, professional experience, from at least the perspective of providing psychological services to abused children and their families, suggests that there are many teachers and education support workers (including classroom assistants, advisory staff, educational psychologists, education social workers) who are soundly planning, developing and implementing a wide variety of counselling services for a wide range of children who have been abused.

Aim of the chapter

Overall, the aim of this chapter is to help those teachers who, across a range of school settings, need to establish a child-centred counselling service, in its broadest sense, for all abused children. The chapter will focus primarily upon preparation for the provision and implementation of counselling services at the whole school and classroom level, but will also include points of relevance about the conditions and features of individual and group counselling programmes. The fundamental intention is to ensure that teachers as counsellors, and as classroom practitioners, are able to interpret and respond to the abused child's feelings and needs.

Raising teachers' awareness

Effective counselling of abused children in schools can only be undertaken by teachers and support staff who are adequately prepared to listen to children's often desperate attempts to relate what are often horrifying experiences. From her work in a schools-based setting Jones (1977) considers how six main elements of typical counselling relationships can usefully be incorporated into teachers' counselling approaches with their pupils. These clearly have particular significance for working with abused children. They should be construed as forming a minimum basis for a teacher's counselling work. In summary, these interpersonal elements are:

● rapport (the necessity for there being a reciprocal need for a counselling realtionship);

- respect for the individual (the need to convey individual worth and self-respect);
- acceptance (the fundamental concern for a genuine and unconditional acceptance);
- empathy (the need to demonstrate understanding of another person's situation and associated feelings);
- trust (the basis upon which the transmission of ideas, thoughts and feelings is constructed and developed);
- confidentiality (the shared agreement to contain any information within the counselling relationship which does not relate to criminal behaviour).

Such features of a counselling relationship between two persons can creatively be translated to form a set of principles underlying effective group work, classroom and whole-school approaches.

The major aim, therefore, for teachers who offer counselling for abused children – and this potentially can mean all teaching staff – has to be the construction of the most effective learning and behavioural environments for their pupils' overall educational and psychological development and which incorporate the above features. To go beyond this brief is likely to cross professional boundaries and to undertake child protection work which might well be the responsibility of someone else. Even though some teachers may well be in specialist positions, where they can offer a range of counselling and therapeutic reponses to individuals or groups of children or strategies more akin to family work undertaken by social workers, these can be successfully implemented only as part of a co-ordinated programme which emanates from a formally held child protection case conference. Good practice in child protection is always a multi-disciplinary endeavour (Stone 1990; DoH, 1991a). That teachers have a highly significant role in children's lives is not in dispute and the Department of Health's (1991b) text on inquiries into children who have been abused easily illustrates this point. However, teachers' professional skills are often under-utilised in the provision of services for children who have been abused. Their potentially highly effective counselling roles need to be emphasised at times such as the proceedings of the child protection case conference. The role of the Designated Member of Staff for Child Protection may well become crucial in this aim (DES 1988).

To make sense of the ways in which their pupils are functioning, teachers develop their own models of children's behaviour. All teachers, whether or not they are formally operating in a counselling role, will need to include in their explanatory models a clear appreciation of how sexual, physical and emotional abuse can significantly affect and reflect children's development. For many teachers this will be a newly encountered perspective on children. In addition to the theoretical explanations of children's behaviour and development, which are more typically encountered in initial and post-experience training, teachers will want continually to appraise and add to their awareness of what is the range and nature of child abuse (Maher, 1987); what it can mean for an abused child to cope with the growing understanding of what has happened to them (Miller, 1990); and what it will take to help them recover from the effects of their traumatic experiences (Johnson, 1989).

Other factors for teachers to be aware of, which are central to effective work in counselling abused children, particularly include:

- the nature of family life (where the majority of all forms of child abuse occurs and which therefore raises significant differences between parents and children's rights, parental responsibilities and children's needs);
- the extent of the variability of parents' abusive behaviour towards their children (including sadistic sexual attacks; psychological torture; food deprivation; deliberate poisoning);
- the significance of social and economic factors underpinning some forms of child abuse and neglect (the greater incidence of parental stress and difficulties in child-rearing in areas of higher unemployment, poverty, and general deprivation);
- the relevance of race, religion, gender and culture in working with abused children (the need to be sensitive to the differing needs of children and families, and to implement effective anti-discriminatory and anti-oppressive strategies);
- the widely varying range of emotional and behavioural difficulties that can beset abused children (especially including the development of overtly sexualised behaviour; sexual identity; self mutilation; suicidal behaviour; eating difficulties such as anorexia and bulimia nervosa; physical aggression and terrorising; extremes of loneliness and feelings of isolation);
- the personal knowledge and experience of abusive events which teachers may have encountered (either personally or via their partners, friends, pupils, and by their contact with pupils' abusing parents).

The statistical background: some comments

Creighton (1987) provides valuable insights into the incidence of child abuse by considering data from the registers of child abuse, between the years of 1977 and 1984, which have been maintained by the National Society for the Prevention of Cruelty to Children (NSPCC). These represent areas totalling about 10 per cent of the child population of England and Wales. Despite definitional changes in the criteria for registering cases of child abuse, certain significant trends are discernible and of importance for teachers. For all the different forms of abuse there were noticeable increases in the percentages of school aged children who had been abused, with the sexual abuse of children providing the greatest increase. Between 5 and 14 years of age, 41 per cent of all cases of child abuse were registered as cases of physical injury.

It is estimated that 58 per cent of all abuse occurs to 5–14 year olds, (26% 5–9; 32% 10–14), with 28 per cent for the 0–4 year olds and 14 per cent for 15–17 year olds. The majority of reported abuse for school aged children for this period (1977–1984) consisted of physical injuries to children (50%). It was noted that younger children were more likely to have received facial and cranial bruising whilst the older school aged children would have received injuries about their body and limbs.

Walton (1989) quotes data which show that of the nearly forty thousand children in England and Wales on child protection registers at the end of March 1988, approximately 25 per cent had been physically abused, 13 per cent sexually abused, and 10 per cent neglected. A third of the children were registered because of 'grave concern'.

However, there are many deficits in such data. Of particular concern to teachers is the age at which children are most likely to suffer different forms of abuse. Research into sexual abuse in Greater Manchester (CSAU, 1988) highlights this problem. Whilst 47 per cent of the study's sample are registered as having been sexually abused when less than 10 years old, 45 per cent had been abused for over a five-year period.

It can be generally concluded however that as the fatal abuse of children has fallen, and the proportion of physically injured has similarly decreased, so the sexual abuse of children has risen dramatically (Creighton, 1987). There were noticeable increases in the percentages of school age children who had been abused physically (from 41% in 1977 to 50% in 1984) or emotionally abused (from 47% in 1982 mean age 5 years 2 months to 67% in 1984 mean age 7 years 6 months).

If data from surveys of the general public (e.g. Baker and Duncan, 1985) are collated alongside other British epidemiological research (e.g. Mrazek, Lynch, and Bentovim, 1981) it is still likely that such figures represent an underestimate of the actual nature of child abuse.

For teachers to design appropriate counselling strategies, and to be able to target particular school populations, they need to be aware of the prevalence rates of the types of abuse according to differing age groups. From the above brief glimpse into statistical data teachers in infant and primary schools are more likely to be involved in the identification and reporting of abused children and thus more directly involved in follow-up work after formal child protection investigations have been completed. Secondary school teachers will need to be prepared for working with children who may have been abused for the first time in their adolescent years but who could have been abused several years beforehand and who are only later able to attempt disclosure.

Whole-school approaches

Counselling for abused children and adolescents is a process which affords a professional context in which those thoughts and feelings that are undermining pupils' sense of self-worth, personal identity and potential for physical development can be examined without judgement, criticism, or a further abuse of the power that always exists in an abusive relationship. Nelson–Jones (1989) succinctly presents the major theories underlying the practice of counselling and offers a useful self-administered questionnaire to help would-be counsellors to explore their theoretical preferences. Teachers are advised to consider the nature of this information in relation to their personal and professional philosophies.

Braun's (1988) work exemplifies the preparation required for an effective whole-school approach. She suggests that there is a need for all children to have opportunities for dealing with trauma by having a curriculum delivered in 'a school with an ethos which empowers children, a school which allows them to voice ideas, opinions and feelings, treats them with respect, values their contributions and treats their families as valued partners in the educational process'. Increasingly, it will be found that the counselling of abused children will be more effective in schools where there has existed an appropriate environment for such services, one which is created from a clearly stated child protection policy. As identified in the DES Circular 4/88 (DES, 1988), the role of the then newly formulated designated member of staff (DMS) for child protection will be central to the overall success of child protection work in schools.

Counselling services for abused children in schools, and policies and practices for child protection, should necessarily be jointly planned with other local agencies, notably the Social Services Department, the Health Authority, and the Police. Children who have been abused should be able to rely upon schools to construct an environment in which the meeting of their particular needs is already an established part of the operational policy of the school, rather than specific problems to be dealt with as if they were unique. One of the most frequently lamented features of abused children's attempts to disclose their abuse, and to receive appropriate support, is that the schools they attended appeared mostly unable to respond to their often urgently stated, although sometimes frequently produced, distress. Schools must demonstrate to all pupils that child protection is fundamentally an adult responsibility, and that children can have recourse to adult support and counselling as a right.

Counselling is clearly an adult-directed activity and is inherently a part of the response of adults towards children in distress. Children ordinarily – at least those who have experienced good-enough care – expect to be comforted and supported following a traumatic event. The fact that abused children are very frequently coerced and variously threatened into remaining silent about their suffering means that their usual pattern of behaviour of going to a trusted adult has been denied them. It is therefore all the more remarkable that some children are able to disclose their abuse. There is no substantial research to indicate what differences there might be in outcome (such as could be measured by assessments of school performance and behaviour, physical health, social and psychological development) between those children who are able to disclose near to the time of abuse and those for whom disclosure occurs long afterwards. But it is known from clinical work with children suffering from post-traumatic stress disorder that where parental, care-giver, or professional (e.g. teacher) support is available soon after the trauma, the positive impact of any counselling and therapeutic approach increases dramatically (Johnson, 1989; Peterson, Prout and Schwarz, 1991).

Peake (Rouf and Peake, 1989) has produced a resource pack of several practice papers, story books and leaflets and provides many valuable suggestions on how it is possible to communicate sensitively and effectively with sexually abused children. The pack gives a practice-based overview of the developmental factors which need to be considered for children of different ages. Of particular note for teachers are her comments about the planning, and the content, of counselling sessions, and of the range of issues which are inescapably a major element of this work (see what is referred to as Paper F). The initial decision to offer a counselling service has to be made, Peake (*ibid.*) says, in a context which offers children obvious support and which forms 'a basis for growth, independence and self help in the future'.

Schools will need to decide on how, at the outset of their planning for a counselling service for their pupils, to target all children who have been, or are at risk of being, maltreated. For those pupils who have yet to disclose the abuse they are experiencing or fearing will happen, this is a critically important distinction. There will also need to be an obvious statement made about the service being different in nature from that which is available for those pupils commonly regarded as presenting troublesome behaviour. Abused children can fall into the latter category but there is enough known about the distress of abused children to suggest that their needs will fundamentally differ in relation to the counselling they can be offered. This must be stated overtly, to allow abused children to identify with a service aimed at meeting their highly specific needs that have arisen as a consequence of harm done to them.

Case study

In working collaboratively with two special school teaching colleagues, Angela Cardwell and Lynn Plimley, on schools-based casework, and in providing training for various groups of mainstream and special needs teachers, it has been possible to provide a range of suggestions for teachers who wish to implement a counselling and therapeutic programme for children who have been abused. Within the aforementioned teachers' own school setting – a multi-racial, day, special school for primary-aged pupils who have a wide variety of learning, emotional and behavioural difficulties – they have produced a useful structure for their classroom-based work. This, in essence, can be transposed into many classrooms, special or mainstream, primary or secondary.

There are six main stages. Each one will be described briefly below so that it will be possible to show how particular skills and perspectives need to be considered and included in a schools-based counselling programme.

1 Some strategies for action

The basis of the work is to allow abused children, whose experiences have significantly contributed to their particular emotional, behavioural and/or learning difficulties (and sometimes physical and medical disabilities) to have as full an access to the National Curriculum as possible. (Robinson (1992) has produced a useful reference for teachers wanting to know how the many different areas of the National Curriculum can be construed within a framework of child protection.) This work is emphasised as being undertaken safely within the security of the school environment where socially and educationally acceptable limits will have been placed upon the disciplinary ethos of the school. Children will necessarily be exposed to essential information about respect for others, the fundamentals of group dynamics, and the overall aim of raising their self-worth to enable their fuller participation in school activities. The construction of universals for the behaviour of adults towards children, and for the children's personal and social behaviour, is central to this work. A charter of adult–child interaction is warranted, as is that for child–child and child–parents, for the school, about home life, and in the community. As stated earlier, such an endeavour must clearly differentiate between children's rights and adults' responsibilities.

2 Developing active listening skills

It is acknowledged that some teachers may have difficulties in listening responsively to their pupils, especially in relation to matters unrelated to school performance and behaviour. There is an overriding need for teachers to implement a model of active listening which can be emulated by pupils. Active listening is a highly developed interpersonal skill which is most successful when operated within a clearly formulated context. The child who has been abused will only accept such an endeavour if it is obvious that the teacher is able to contain and manage those details which the child wishes to discuss. What teachers should remember is that abused children are often able to discriminate between those adults who will be able to provide effective support and those who will not - although bear in mind the points made earlier about children's attempts to tell their teachers of the abuse they had suffered. Abused children rightly become highly despondent when an adult begins to listen to their distress but then backs away, very often for reasons unstated to the child.

Where it is possible, a specific structure is required, whether for the whole class, a small group or individuals. This could include a set time each day, in each class. Ground rules have to be established. Thus:

- children will need to be given permission to use language which is appropriate to them (sometimes including expletives and sexually explicit words, where these clearly arise out of abusive situations);
- children will need to hear teachers sincerely supporting, by patience and positive reinforcement, ill-articulated or poorly expressed contributions;
- children will want assurances that what they may say will not be greeted with derision or incomprehension, and this means teachers must be very well aware of their non-verbal behaviour too, because abused children often have highly developed skills for perceiving the moods and feelings of others;
- children must be clear that their teachers are not merely awaiting a disclosure; they need to know that their other concerns and problems, directly or indirectly related to abuse, can also be exchanged.

Initiating this work need not be problematic. Given an appropriate structure, simple statements likely to generate much comment can be produced by teachers to encourage children to think of personal circumstances and of those which might affect people they know (including those featured in the media, in television, and within their local community or school). There will need to be a balance between positive and negative examples to enable children to explore a range of situations and emotions. Where children have specific speech, and possibly language and sensory difficulties, teachers will need to construct a framework of symbolic and interpretative behaviour within which children can seek to communicate their contribution.

3 Raising self-esteem

This is an area of psychological development which is especially vital to those children who have suffered abuse. Not only should teachers offer abused children repeated opportunities to experience a positive assessment and promotion of their self-understanding, but they must equally provide them with the means for developing their own strategies which could contribute to raising their self-esteem. Teachers are in a central position to ensure that a uniform approach is being developed. Where appropriate, parents and significant carers should be encouraged by teachers to report in front of their children on the positive examples of their behaviour and development. It is sometimes difficult to provide meaningful rewards to promote the increase or decrease of specific aspects of children's behaviour but teachers', and pupils', self-created reinforcement schedules can be utilised to aid this process. The overall aim of self-reward, from the children's measurement and evaluation of their own successes, will need to be carefully explained and exemplified.

4 Using prevention programmes

Many schools use child abuse prevention programmes within the general context of promoting rules for personal safety – whether this relates to accident prevention at home or school; living healthily, physically and psychologically; or the wide-ranging factors of environmental protection. In each case, the aim is to give children the opportunity to rehearse appropriate coping strategies for their own protection and the exercising of their rights to express their dislike of certain situations. Whilst it is necessary to seek permission from governors, parents and the children to cover intimate and sometimes unlikeable topics, there must also be an overt attempt to balance inputs with a consideration of developmental factors. Many schemes exist for children of all ages: for the younger child, Toby and the Gang (Adams and Gifford, 1992) is a most suitable example to use with 3–8 year olds. It has also been used successfully with individuals and small groups of children who have been abused and who require specific counselling to enable them to develop their skills sufficiently to feel that they are no longer defenceless. Kidscape (1986) is pre-eminent for primary-aged children, while Teenscape (Kidscape, 1990) and work by Adams, Foy and Lorean–Martin (1988) are suitable resources for teachers working with younger and older adolescents.

5 Developing trust and safety

Many abused children suffer a profound loss of faith in people as a consequence of having been abused. This is more likely as they come to acknowledge what roles abusing parents should have undertaken had they been providing appropriate care. To expect that trust and feelings of safety will develop easily is to be misguided (Fong and Gresbach Cox, 1983). Teachers will be helping any abused child by not expecting overt signs of being trusted or of feeling safe. Given the shocking nature of abusive experiences certain children may never be able to develop these features in their school lives. What teachers can ensure, irrespective of the disclosure of abuse, is the promotion of the positive values of what is predictable and safe about the routines of school life. There is also much to be gained from exemplifying the benefits of not trusting adults too much, of how to be aware of relationships which allow one person undue control and power. When dealing specifically with the avoidance of abusive relationships it is necessary, sensitively, to illustrate the ways in which some adults, and older children, seek to coerce their juniors into situations in which they expect submission and collusion with unwanted and abusive behaviours. The information that perpetrators of child sexual abuse have provided is especially revealing about the expertise many sexual offenders have in terms of their ability to target, befriend, and groom children for abuse, and thus capitalise upon the child's vulnerability. Teachers need to comprehend the amount of planning that is central to the majority of sexual assaults, whether within the family or the community (and this, sadly, includes professional carers, teachers, and other workers).

6 Self-evaluation

All children have a basic need to understand how they are progressing in relation to the efforts they make at school. This is just as true for those children who have been abused, and who often have a desperate need to know how they are developing as a consequence of their attempts, both in trying to change their thinking and their behaviour, in relation to the abuse they have experienced. Realistic counselling – for individuals, groups, whole classes, even the whole school – will best proceed if appropriate goals are negotiated for discrete aspects of children's behaviour. The most effective way of evaluation, as Sutton (1987) practically explains, is to undertake this in four stages:

(1) *Building relationships and a preliminary assessment of the difficulties*
   This obviously requires an overt child protection policy within the school sufficient for those children who have been abused to

feel confident to disclose or, at least, to know that their problems are comprehended.

(2) *Negotiating and agreeing goals as perceived by the clients*
Again, this can proceed on an individual basis with children who are known to have been abused or, more systemically, across the class or whole school, as a means of being proactive in creating a context for the better understanding of the needs of any child who has suffered a traumatic experience.

(3) *Intervention*
As in the application of specific counselling strategies, as a means of moving towards goals agreed with the clients.

(4) *Evaluation*
By various means, formal and informal, client-constructed and counsellor constructed, of the extent to which goals have been achieved.

In whatever way the evaluation is structured, it must be personalised to suit the needs of those for whom the counselling is being provided. Depending upon the age and, where appropriate, the cognitive and fine-motor-skills of the children concerned, various forms of graphical representation can be used. Where the counselling approach utilises written and practical work this can be exhibited, and accompanied by suitably-phrased commentaries. More advanced, whole-school counselling approaches, as part of a preventive programme, can make use of, for example, systems designed to evaluate the quality of interpersonal relationships; the amount of communal help displayed; and the positive interventions children and young people have made to improve the emotional environment and physical and psychological safety of the school or class.

Innovatively, in the context of helping children's peer group relationships, peer courts can be established to determine rewards and punishments to suit the accomplishment or misbehaviour. Much can be understood about children's views of each other's behaviour when they are given the right of jurisdiction. The children's decision-making can be examined for their sense of moral and social sense of justice. Such practice clearly allows for parallels to be provided between how teachers treat their pupils and how parents relate to their children. Roscoe (1990) found that adolescents were, in general, harshly critical of parents who maltreated their children. In his research different vignettes were used to depict various examples of child abuse, for a range of levels of seriousness in relation to 7-year old children. The adolescent subjects were asked to use a nine point rating scale to indicate their feelings about the inappropriateness or otherwise of parental behaviour towards their children. Such an exercise can usefully be modified for educational purposes with a range of pupils.

Conclusions and recommendations

A school-based counselling service for abused children, irrespective of the age range of pupils, or type of educational provision being offered, will best be promoted by teachers who have undertaken a wide range of training exercises to prepare themselves for the horrific experiences that abused children have encountered. Teachers will need to have wide-ranging discussions about how to design and develop a variety of interventions relevant to:

- individual children who have been abused, or are at risk of being abused;
- classroom work;
- whole school approaches;
- working with parents;
- involvement with members of the local community;
- school governors.

Cicchetti, Toth and Hennessy (1989) discuss the developmental consequences of child abuse in relation to schooling. They suggest that there are five main principles to be considered when planning to meet the educational needs of abused children; especially within the context of how abuse affects the development of relationships, self-esteem, and cognitive functioning in general:

(1) *Least delay*
    The chances of lessening the damage of abuse are heightened the sooner the intervention is provided after the abuse has been identified.
(2) *Maximising the educational environment*
    This may include special programmes of individual and group therapy/counselling; introducing curriculum materials and classroom activities which are designed to er.hance pupils perceptions of their own cognitive and social competence.
(3) *Parental involvement*
    As an aim to modify parent–child interaction there is a need to

facilitate parents' understanding of child development and positive forms of management.
(4) *Developmental perspectives*
To ensure the promotion of age-appropriate competencies across the whole curriculum.
(5) *Continuous professional development*
Especially in relation to the conseqences of child abuse.

For teachers and schools to be optimally effective in the implementation of their counselling services there is a necessary requirement to consider how to meet the range of needs that abused children can present when at school. This is especially relevant when in relation to social, psychological, developmental and educational factors. Clearly, the counselling to be offered must reflect the children's age; their gender; their ethnic, religious and cultural background; any known physical or sensory disability, learning or communication difficulty; and whether or not they attend a mainstream or special school.

Of added significance to the counselling process are other factors related to the abusing behaviour:

● the type of abuse that has been experienced (was it emotional, physical, or sexual abuse; or neglect?);
● the source of the abuse (did this occur from within the child's family; the community; or the school?);
● other specific aspects of the relationship between the child and the person(s) who perpetrated the abuse (e.g. if the abuse occurred outside the child's family was the perpetrator known to the child; was the child required to give evidence as a witness in criminal or care proceedings; was the child removed from the family home to local authority accommodation; was the child abused as part of a group activity?); and
● the shared knowledge of the abuse (who knows about what happened to the child; has the child informed his/her peers; has the child attended any therapeutic/counselling services external to the school?).

Finally, whilst all teachers need to be particularly aware of how their pupils' sense of self-worth and self-identity can be variously affected by abuse, this will differ significantly according to the children's age. However, any child who is abused, irrespective of age or the nature of the abuse, will come to feel disempowered at some stage in their development. It may not be that, immediately following or during an abusive episode, a child will gain any sense of themselves as being diminished. This is because, as Miller (1990) forcefully states, all children who are being abused will need to repress the full horror of such experiences simply to continue existing. The perpetrators of abuse almost always seek to silence their victims by coercing them in to believing that what is happening to them is either necessary for their development or is being done to them because that is a way of showing them that they are being loved. The whole basis of abused children's abilities to form realtionships is therefore constantly being undermined by such deliberate distortions of the perpetrators' relationship with their victims. Perpetrators seek to exert and maintain control over their victims. They can only continue to abuse if this feeling of dominance is present in their abusive relationship.

Many children who have been abused will clearly demonstrate their feelings of powerlessness and inadequacy in their interpersonal relationships within the school setting. Typical examples of behaviours will more often than not directly reflect the abusive relationship to which they have been, or are being, subjected. There will, therefore, be an infinite variety of ways in which abused children will interact with their peers, teachers, and younger/older pupils. However, what characterises such interactions, and what forms a main focus for teachers' counselling approaches with abused children, of whatever age, is their attempt to reduce the significance of others whom they encounter. The abused child is straightforwardly deflecting onto others the hostility, pain, degradation, and abasement that has been experienced within their own abusive context. Having had to assume a submissive role with the perpetrator of their own abuse, abused children at some stage will invariably – if not during their school career then in their later years – seek in many varying ways to adopt a more controlling role of their own. The nature of this reaction will differ considerably, but it is highly correlated with gender. This is most starkly revealed when contemplating the sexual abuse of children, as the majority of reports of child sexual abuse illustrate how more girls than boys are abused (although there are likely to be significant factors relating to the under-reporting of sexual abuse to boys). However, the abuse is overwhelmingly by males. It is only necessary to consider the far greater number of male perpetrators, of all forms of abuse, to realise that child abuse is essentially a massive problem related directly to masculinity, and male sexuality in particular.

Of chief concern to the counselling process is the promotion in abused children of the recognition that their relationships will have invariably suffered as a direct consequence of having been abused. For children to be given a context in which it is possible to have it stated that their sometimes destructive interactions with others are related to events over which they have had no control, nor were in any way responsible for, can be one of the most comforting and supporting statements to be made. Abused children have to be helped to recognise that, in their future dealings with people, often at a variety of levels, they will need to be aware of the strategies they employ in their interactions. Teachers who offer well-prepared, sensitively implemented counselling approaches are pre-eminently placed to be of life-long value to abused children. The recognition of this role is long overdue.

References

Adams, C., Foy, J. and Lorean–Martin, J. (1984) *NO is not enough: Helping teenagers avoid sexual assault*. San Luis Obispo, CA: Impact Publishers.

Adams, J. and Gifford, V. (1992) *Taking care with Toby and the Puppet Gang*. Nuneaton: George Elliot Hospital, N.E. Warwickshire Health Authority.

Baker, A.W. and Duncan, S. (1985) 'Child sexual abuse: A study of prevalence in Great Britain'. *Child Abuse and Neglect*, 9.

Braun, D. (1988) *Responding to child abuse: Action and planning for teachers and other professionals*. London: Bedford Square Press.

Child Sexual Abuse Unit (1988) 'Child sexual abuse in Greater Manchester: A regional profile' in: C. Wattam, J. Hughes and H. Blagg (eds) (1989) *Child sexual abuse: Listening, hearing and validating the experiences of children*. Harlow: Longman.

Cicchetti, D., Toth, S.L. and Hennessy, K. (1989) 'Research on the consequences of child maltreatment and its application to educational settings'. *Topics in Early Childhood Special Education*, **9**, (2), pp. 33–55.

Creighton, S.J. (1987) 'Quantitative assessment of child abuse' in: P. Maher (ed) (1987) *Child abuse: The educational perspective*. Oxford: Blackwell.

Department of Education and Science (1988) Circular 4/88: *Working together for the protection of children from abuse: Procedures within the education service*.

Department of Health (1991a) *Working together: A guide to arrangements for inter-agency cooperation for the protection of children*. London: HMSO.

Department of Health (1991b) *Child abuse: A study of inquiry reports 1980–1989*. London: HMSO.

Fong, M.L. and Gresbach Cox, B. (1983) 'Trust as an underlying dynamic in the counselling process: How clients test trust'. *Personnel and Guidance Counselling*, **62**, pp, 163–166.

Johnson, K. (1989) *Trauma in the lives of children*. Basingstoke, England: Macmillan.

Jones, A. (1977) *Counselling adolescents in school*. London: Kogan Page.

Kidscape (1986) *Kidscape Primary Kit*. London: Kidscape Ltd.

Kidscape (1990) *Teenscape: Personal safety programme for young people*. London: Kidscape Ltd.

Maher, P. (ed) (1987) *Child abuse: The educational perspective*. Oxford: Blackwell.

Miller, A. (1990) *Banished knowledge: Facing childhood injuries*. London: Virago Press.

Mrazek, P., Lynch, M. and Bentovim, A. (1981) 'A recognition of child sexual abuse in the United Kingdom' in: P. Mrazek and C. H. Kempe (eds) (1981) *Sexually abused children and their families*. London: Pergamon.

Nelson–Jones, R. (1989) *Practical counselling skills*. London: Holt, Rinehart and Winston.

Peterson, K. C., Prout, M. F. and Schwarz, R. A. (1991) *Post-traumatic stress disorder: A clinician's guide*. New York: Plenum Press.

Robinson, G. (1992) *Child protection in the National Curriculum*. Birmingham: Health Education Unit, Birmingham Local Education Authority.

Roscoe, B. (1990) Defining child maltreatment: Ratings of parental behaviours. *Adolescence*, **25**, 99 (Fall) pp. 517–528.

Rouf, K. and Peake, A. (1989) *Working with sexually abused children: A resource pack for professionals*. London: Children's Society.

Stone, M. (1990) *Child protection work: A professional guide*. Birmingham: Venture Press.

Sutton, C. (1987) 'The evaluation of counselling: A goal-attainment approach'. *Counselling*, **60**, pp. 14–20.

Walton, M. (1989) 'What use are statistics? Policy and practice in child abuse' in: C. Wattam, J. Hughes and H. Blagg. (eds) (1989) *Child sexual abuse: Listening, hearing and validating the experiences of children*. Harlow: Longman.

CHAPTER 6

Putting Problems in Context – the Family and the School

Graham Upton

Behaviour problems are the concern of all educators. In this chapter Graham Upton explores the systemic approach, which focuses on the context of the classroom, school, family and even society on resolving difficulties. This is a challenge to traditional approaches in working with children and young people in schools, which has been a child-centred view of behaviour.

In schools there is a tendency to conceptualise difficulties in behaviour and learning in ways whereby the pupil is seen as being, or having, the problem. For the teacher concerned with establishing an effective learning environment for a whole class of children or young people, the pupil who does not participate easily in classroom activities, the pupil who disrupts those activities and the pupil who fails to learn from them is a pupil without whom life would clearly be easier and more rewarding. Working from the assumption that education in general, and schools in particular, are positively good features of our society, historical attempts to understand and intervene with problems such as these have traditionally focused on the individual in isolation from the immediate context of the classroom and school and the broader context of family and society.

   Children and young people have been variously labelled as

educationally sub-normal and maladjusted or as having learning difficulties and emotional and behavioural problems. Intervention has ranged from temporary withdrawal from their ordinary class for counselling and remedial teaching to more permanent placement in a special class, unit or school. The objective specialist help has invariably been the remediation of the pupils' difficulties in order that they will be able to respond more appropriately to the requirements of classroom life. Thus, in his now classic work on school counselling Hamblin (1978) writes that 'the counsellor is concerned with the understanding and prevention of alienation and the production of attitudes which allow pupils to avail themselves of the resources of the school'.

While such individual ascription of blame and individualised approach to intervention is understandable, it ignores much of what we know about the nature of behaviour and learning problems in schools and fails to address the limitations of such an approach to intervention.

Why should problems be viewed in their context?

There are several reasons why we need to look at both behaviour and learning problems in a broad context.

(1) Schools and individual teachers vary enormously in what they regard as acceptable behaviour. Whether pupils are seen as having behaviour problems depends as much on the school in which they are pupils and on the particular teachers with whom they are in contact as it does on the actual behaviour which the pupils exhibit. Thus, a pupil who fails to wear school uniform may be seen as presenting a more serious challenge to the values and attitudes of the school if, for example, that school was a grant maintained school striving to improve its image amongst parents, rather than an 11–16 comprehensive faced with problems of severe social deprivaiton where such an issue may be seen as inconsequential. In other words it is not the behaviour *per se* which is problematic but where it occurs and how it is perceived in that situation. Any attempt to intervene in that situation should logically address the context as well as the behaviour.

(2) Behaviour in schools is frequently situation-specific and it is common for pupils to behave very differently from one class to the next, and from one teacher to the next. This applies equally

to learning difficulties where marked differences in achievement between subject areas frequently characterise the performance of pupils. It is possible to see this as being determined solely by the pupil but more accurately it must be seen as reflecting different sets of interactions between the pupil and the teachers involved, and the different ways in which whole groups of pupils behave in different situations. Equally, it is important to understand that not all teachers find it easy to establish positive relationships with 'difficult' pupils. Thus, it is important to consider where behaviour and learning problems occur and to identify the different roles played by the individual, the peer group and teachers who are involved in their occurrence.

(3) Behaviour at home is frequently very different from that at school. This is in line with the situation-specific nature of behaviour referred to above but also frequently reflects differences between parents and teachers in their attitudes towards what constitutes good and bad behaviour. Aggressive or violent behaviour, for example, might be considered unacceptable by teachers and society at large but may well constitute a norm in the family and within the family's social network. Failure to see the 'problem' in context could be counter-productive to any attempt to modify a pupil's behaviour in school and could create an even greater divide between the family and the school.

(4) Behaviour problems in school often reflect underlying emotional difficulties whereby pupils can be seen to be acting out severe emotional difficulties, the origins of which lie within the disturbing experiences of their family life. Recently, the importance of this has been highlighted in relation to problems of sexual and physical abuse (Hall, 1992) but the concept has long provided a rationale for the placement of children and young people in residential special schools. While such problems can be responded to as individual difficulties they can only be fully understood in the context of the interpersonal dynamics of the family where they originate.

(5) The study of school differences has suggested that teachers and schools too must be seen as a potential causative factors in the occurrence of behaviour and learning problems (Rutter *et al.*, 1979; Reynolds, 1976, 1984). Until recently there has been an imbalance in the understanding of educational problems which has emphasised matters of individual and family pathology and environmental deprivation and ignored the differences which

clearly exist between schools and teachers in creating effective learning environments. Yet it is abundantly clear to parents, for example, that some schools are 'better' than others and it would be professionally dishonest to suggest that all teachers possessed an equally high level of teaching competence. If this is accepted then it is inappropriate to focus all our attention on the individual pupil when trying to understand the difficulties that pupil is experiencing in school. We need, for example, to recognise the role which the school's academic and management systems might be playing in the generation of a learning or behaviour problem and to acknowledge the necessity to focus intervention sometimes on the teacher rather than the pupil.

Thinking in terms of systems

Support for the argument that pupils' behaviour needs to be considered in terms of its context has been provided by the development of theories and practices of psychotherapy and counselling which emphasise the interactional nature of behavioural patterns. Psychodynamic theorists and practitioners (e.g. Brown and Pedder, 1979) and behaviourally oriented writers (e.g. Wheldall and Glynn, 1989) have long emphasised the importance of interactions in the generation of emotional and behavioural difficulties, as have humanistically oriented psychotherapists such as Rogers (1951) who have been so influential in the development of counselling both in schools and with adults.

In spite of their recognition of the importance of interactions in the development of problems the orientation of most of the traditional schools of psychotherapy and counselling has primarily been with the individual. However, in recent years alternative approaches have been developed which have a more direct focus on the systems of which the individual is part. This type of thinking has had a significant influence on the work of the educational psychologist (Campion, 1985) but the recent growth of family therapy represents a more complete application of systemic thinking and there now exists a substantive body of literature and research which demonstrates the efficacy of systemic approaches in the treatment of a wide range of psychiatric disorders and emotional and behavioural difficulties (for a general introduction to the theory and practice of family therapy readers are referred to Burnham, 1986).

However, the application of these ideas in British schools in general, and in relation to school counselling in particular, has been slow. While American workers (Amatea, 1989; Molnar and Lindquist, 1989) have provided substantive evidence of their value in dealing with a wide range of school-based behaviour problems their use in Britain has been more limited. Nonetheless, good examples of their potential do exist. Family therapists working with educationalists (Dowling and Osborne, 1985) have illustrated the ways in which behaviour and learning difficulties in schools can be symptomatic of dysfunctions in the family system, the school system and in the family–school relationship system, and have provided good case study material to support the effectiveness of intervention based on systemic principles.

The ecosystemic approach

A framework for the application of systemic thinking to the understanding and treatment of behaviour problems in schools has been provided by the development of what has come to be termed the **ecosystemic approach**. The principles of this approach have been enunciated by Upton and Cooper (1990) and Cooper and Upton (1990a), and its relevance to pastoral care and school counselling by Cooper and Upton (1990b), but its key components can be summarised in terms of four statements, viz:

(1) Problem behaviour in the classroom does not originate from within the individual who displays the behaviour, but from within the interaction between that individual and other individuals.

(2) Interactional patterns may be conceptualised in simple or complex ways. A simple analysis is confined to here-and-now situations, and will define a student's negative behaviour in terms of the interactions in the classroom which immediately surround the behaviour. A complex analysis will take into account factors in the wider ecosystem and explore purposes which the here-and-now behaviour might serve in other, related ecosystems. Such an analysis may relate oppositional behaviour in the classroom to interactional patterns in the student's family or include broader considerations within the school.

(3) The cause of any instance of problem behaviour is part of a cyclical chain of actions and reactions between participants. Each event in an interactional chain can be seen as both a cause of ensuing events and the effect of preceding events depending where we choose to 'punctuate' the chain. Furthermore, student

classroom behaviour which is defined as 'problematic' is always goal directed and, from the student's viewpoint, it is understandable, rational and, above all, necessary. What appears problematic to the teacher may well be the solution to a problem for the student, for a subsystem in the classroom or school, or the student's family.

(4) Intervention strategies must be based on a recognition of the contribution made to a problem situation by all participating parties in the interaction surrounding the problem. Thus, in a classroom the teacher and the other children in the class must be seen to contribute to the generation of the particular behaviour problem as much as the child or children concerned. Each is equally involved and each may thus be the focus of intervention.

In sum, the central focus of the approach is on understanding behaviour problems in schools in terms of the interactions of the persons involved, either within the school situation or in related contexts (such as the family of the pupil concerned, the staff group etc.).

Putting the ecosystemic approach into practice

For most teachers and in most schools thinking in terms of systems is not common primarily because it rejects the tendency to ascribe blame to individual pupils and puts in its place a model which necessitates a more balanced evaluation of the contributions made by all the people who 'contribute' to its occurrence. As such, however, it is in keeping with the wealth of research evidence which illustrates the ways in which schools, individual teachers and families influence the behaviour and learning of pupils. But, clearly, such an approach can be threatening to teachers and parents in that it requires them to recognise that their influence on the pupil may be negative. This is something which neither teachers nor parents find easy and great sensitivity is needed in introducing such a contextually oriented approach.

Working with colleagues

An ecosystemic analysis of conflict within schools, whether it be between teacher and pupil, pupil and pupil or teacher and teacher, invariably reveals individuals or groups pursuing different goals and ignoring, denying or opposing the validity of others' goals, with the results that opposition leads to entrenchment and continually escalating conflict. The ecosystemic solution to such conflict is to look for explanations which do not apportion blame or guilt and which lead to the development of cooperative relationships between the individuals concerned. Teachers, thus, need to be encouraged to develop an emphatic understanding of pupils with whom they come into conflict, as a means of gaining a critical insight into their own behaviour. Empathy itself becomes a form of cooperation which, at once, is both disarming to a potential opponent as well as providing encouragement for an open and harmonious relationship. Equality and cooperation, however, do not always characterise relationships within schools or between schools and parents, and care needs to be taken when working with colleagues to avoid the approach as being seen as a threat to their status as teachers.

There are many specific ways in which such an approach can be applied in schools but a technique described by Molnar and Lindquist (1989) as 'reframing' illustrates clearly how such principles can be put into practice. This technique is based on four propositions which, in combination, can help colleagues move towards a balanced understanding of conflict in the classroom and the broader context of the school. These are:

(1) In a conflict situation we behave in accordance with our interpretation of that situation.
(2) There are often many different but equally valid interpretations of any given situation.
(3) If we change our interpretation we can change our behaviour.
(4) Change in our behaviour will influence the perceptions and behaviours of others, particularly if we break out of a pattern of behaviour which has become predictable.

To illustrate these ideas Molnar and Lindquist use the example of a child repeatedly calling out answers in class. In this situation a common reaction of teachers is to consider the behaviour as inappropriate attention seeking and to ignore it. The pupil's view can offer a very different perspective and it is conceivable, for example, as Molnar and Lindquist suggest, that children may call out because they believe that the teacher tends to ignore them. Such differing perceptions can lead to children and teachers becoming locked in a vicious circle of calling out and ignoring. In this type of situation reframing can be a simple and effective means of breaking the vicious circle that has developed. This would require the teacher to see the situation differently and on the basis of this perception to change his or her behaviour accordingly. Thus, if the teacher could be helped to re-interpret the student's calling out positively as reflecting involvement and interest, or perhaps as anxiety to please the teacher, rather than negative attention seeking then the teacher may be able to evolve other ways of responding to the child than ignoring. Such a positive interpretation frees the teacher to initiate changes in the situation by behaving differently, which change will, in due course, necessitate a change in the child's behaviour.

Such a strategy will not, of course, produce instant results. It will also need to be given time to work. The pupil will have to be convinced of the genuineness of the teacher's reframing, and be confident that this is not an example of teacher sarcasm or 'kidology'. Achieving this will require a willingness on the teacher's part to persevere beyond the initial trial of the method. It will also require a good understanding of the strategy and its underlying rationale and it will be necessary to consider specialist training for staff if such strategies are to be used effectively. It will in addition be necessary for at least one member of staff to have sufficient knowledge of the approach to act as consultant to other members of staff; a person who is highly skilled in ecosystemic analysis and who can function on a 'meta' level as consultant to both teachers and pupils. Consideration might also profitably be given to the development of a staff support group. Such a group can help facilitate alternative interpretations of problematic situations, especially those where the teacher is a key participant, and to provide help with determining intervention strategies as well as a source of encouragement for the continued exploration of the use of the approach.

If the approach is successful there can be far reaching consequences for the quality of the teacher–pupil relationships in a school, and these may evolve into a new found spirit of cooperation, with concomitantly positive effects on the quality of classroom relationships generally (see Molnar and Lindquist, 1989). Another important outcome is the influence such an approach has on the development of a reflective approach by teachers to their classroom practice. It is suggested that the type of self monitoring advocated here is as important as the pupil monitoring common in behavioural approaches to classroom disruption.

Working with parents

The principles outlined above in relation to the use of the ecosystemic approach within schools can be readily transferred for use with parents and families. However, if attempts are to be made to work systemically with parents the general climate which exists in the school in relation to home–school relationships is vitally important. Since the Plowden Report recommended that all primary schools should have a programme for contact with children's homes the need for good parent–teacher relationships has become a *sine qua non* in nearly all areas of education. In special education the concept of 'parents as partners', which was introduced in the Warnock Report, has become a catchword and more recently parents have been given significant rights in regard to their children's education under the 1991 Education Act and 1988 Education Reform Act. In practice, however, the rhetoric and reality are often far apart. While some schools operate an 'open door' policy and work hard to encourage parental interest and involvement others seem covertly (if not overtly) hostile to parents, especially with regards to parents whose children present learning and behavioural difficulties. The experience of a student teacher as described by Sewell (1986) is unfortunately all to familiar:

> The teachers in her primary school used to gather at the staffroom window every morning, watching parents bring their children to school. They would make cutting remarks about how parents treated their children or how they dressed. They were particulalry scathing about the parents of those who gave them the most trouble, those with learning or behaviour difficulties.

To engage in 'therapeutic' interaction with parents in this situation would clearly be extremely difficult. The task is not made any easier by a tendency, even in schools where more positive attitudes towards parents exist, for school/parent contact to be uni-directional (from school to parents) and primarily concerned with imparting information to parents rather than working with them in any real sense of partnership. At the same time, and in fairness to schools and teachers, it must also be acknowledged that it is often difficult for schools to make more than token contacts with parents because of the limited time which staff can realistically devote to this aspect of their work and the fact that, even in situations where an open door policy operates, contact with parents frequently focuses on the parents of the more able and the highly motivated, because the parents whom teachers really want to see simply don't respond to initiatives to involve them. Not all parents are willing (and able) to co-operate readily with the school. This is probably particularly true in relation to behavioural problems where, as was noted above, the problem presented by the pupil in school may originate from family difficulties or differences in attitudes and values between the home and school.

The role of the consultant

When faced with problems where the family is seen as having a major responsibility for the generation and maintenance of a problem, either because of the existence of serious family conflict or where there is a strong element of parental–school conflict, it is advisable to utilise the skills of an expert consultant with teachers and school very much in the role of client. An example of the effective use of a consultant is provided by Power and Bartholomew (1985), who present a case study involving a student with learning and behaviour difficulties and in which parent–school enmity was a significant issue. After a period of sustained conflict between the school and family, a family therapist was brought in as a consultant. From his position the therapist was able to develop an interpretation of the situation which the involvement of the teachers would have made it almost impossible for them to do.

In brief this 'meta' analysis suggested that while the teachers were concerned to overcome the pupil's learning difficulties, his parents appeared to be using their son's difficulties as a diversion from their marital problems. In their concern for their son's problems the parents were able to unite with one another and this helped to prevent marital break-up. As a result the parents had a vested interest in maintaining their son's difficulties and did so by opposing the school's efforts to solve their son's problems through, for instance, over-protectiveness and encouraging him not to complete homework assignments. Teachers at the school responded to what they saw as family collusion by being unsympathetic towards the student and making further demands upon him.

The family therapist saw this pattern of school–family interaction as being characterised by a pattern of symmetrical interaction, 'that is, one in which each party responds to what the other is doing in a similar way' whereby the parents and teachers were locked in constant competition for the dominant position. Thus, the teachers' suggestion that the student's school problems were related to family circumstances would be met by the counterclaim that the teachers were not working effectively. It is the nature of such relationships to escalate, leading to deeper entrenchment on both sides, with each party undermining the efforts made by the other to help the student. Ironically, the chief loser was, of course, the student.

Without assistance from an outsider a solution to the student's difficulties would seem unlikely to emerge from such a conflict. The consultant, however, was able to propose an intervention which sought to convert this symmetrical relationship into a more positive complementary relationship characterised by non-competitive interaction. The strategy which was devised was subtle and simple. To begin with the consultant persuaded the school staff to resist argument and to be compliant with the parents' views at the next meeting. When, during the meeting, the parents became hostile towards the school staff, the consultant took up the parental position and presented it in exaggerated form, suggesting that their son should be relieved of all pressure in class. Paradoxically, the parents resisted this and responded to it in a contradictory manner arguing that 'the teacher did have the right to place some expectations on the students in her class'. This was the point at which the staff and parents were in agreement for the first time. The deadlock was broken and an opportunity to develop a collaborative relationship was established.

The eventual outcome of the case was that the parents and the school staff agreed to recognise the primacy of each other in their respective domains. The teachers agreed not to pressure the student in class and, instead of setting specific homework tasks in addition to classwork, they agreed to allow him to take uncompleted classwork home. Further, it was agreed that whether he completed the tasks at home was a matter for the parents to decide and the school would simply award the appropriate grade without placing any pressure on the student. By allowing the student to take classwork home, the school was enabling the parents to control the pressure which was placed on their son. This newly collaborative relationship between the school and the family also led to their accepting advice from a psychologist on aiding their son with stress management. Thus, the student's therapeutic needs were met, as were the parents' needs for a collaborative activity with one another (i.e. as a diversion from their marital difficulties) and the school's position was also validated.

To some extent the reason why consultants can be effective in situations such as this is partly explained by the opportunity which their position as outsider provides for them to obtain a meta perspective of the situation. But it also clearly depends on their therapeutic skill and there are clearly dangers for schools in embarking on such 'delicate' work with parents without appropriate support.

Teachers working independently

For the most part, learning and behaviour problems do not involve a high degree of family pathology and there are many situations in schools when teachers can work within a systemic framework with parents supported either by a specially trained member of staff or within the context of a peer support group (the value of which was noted above in relation to school-based problems). This suggestion does not, of course, deny any role for additional specialist support. Specialist consultants who are external to the school can provide valuable advice and support even when only limited access to them is available, as well as sometimes being able to provide supervision for individual teachers and input to a staff support group.

There are many features of current practice in schools which involve interaction between teachers and parents and it is possible to utilise these to devise practicable ways in which teachers can work therapeutically with parents.

(1) In responding to learning and behavioural difficulties schools commonly invite parents to come to the school to discuss problems but such contact can be initiated by the parents. Often the session is conducted solely by a single member of staff but the involvement of teachers and staff external to the school, such as social workers and educational psychologists, is common. The value of this approach is that it requires limited resources, it can be initiated quickly by parents or school staff, it brings the parents into the school and can facilitate the school and parents working together in quite intensive ways. It does, however, have disadvantages. Parents can feel unequal on school territory and feel that they have been victimised/singled out for special treatment. Often too only the mother can come during school hours and travelling to school can create problems for some parents.

(2) In some schools staff take on part of the traditional role of the social worker and visit children's homes to work with parents. This is sometimes formalised with the appointment of a teacher-social worker. The advantages of this are that the interaction takes place on the parents' territory and can result in them feeling more at ease and more willing to enter into meaningful

dialogue. It also allows the teacher to see something of the child's behaviour at home and gain some direct insight into actual home conditions, which knowledge can be used to facilitate the development of programmes to use at home based on advice from the school. On the negative side it is not always practical in terms of the demands it makes on school staffing and the special skills which staff should have to undertake this work.

(3) A variation on the idea of school staff visiting the homes of individual children is for groups of parents who live close to one another to meet with school staff on a regular basis as a discussion group. Issues of general concern can be dealt with effectively in this way and if a positive group atmosphere is generated specific issues related to individual children and families can also be addressed. The fact that the interaction takes place on the parents' territory is a positive feature of this way of work, but more important perhaps is the way in which it fosters the sharing of problems between parents. Some parents can gain enormous confidence from working in a group and can establish a more equal relationship with school staff than they might otherwise be able to do. Such groups can also foster relationships between parents and generate an ethos of self-help and the shared solution of problems. Unsocial hours for school staff can be a problem and parents may easily opt out while careful leadership is needed to ensure that sessions do not degenerate into aimless chat sessions.

(4) On a more didactic level teaching/learning workshops for parents can be organised to focus on specific issues such as behavioural management, reading, or play activities. There are many ways in which workshops can be organised but commonly parents come to school for a pre-determined number of sessions in which they participate in a structured teaching programme. These are usually conducted out of school hours but if conducted in school time have the added advantage of involvement of the children. Ideally staff participate alongside the parents to ensure home and school are working in the same direction. A particular benefit of these activities is that they provide parents with advice and guidance that is often sorely lacking. The didactic nature of the activities and the fact that they involve group activity can also foster feelings of security and paradoxically allow parents to share problems more directly than they might be willing to do when that is a more explicit expectation of the group.

(5)   A Home/School diary which travels with the child from home to school has been found by many schools to provide a valuable means of communication between parents and teachers. In this way teachers and parents can cooperate on specific activities, teachers can keep parents informed of progress in schools, methods being used, etc. and parents can keep school informed of events at home, problems experienced, etc.

(6)   Formal events such as open days and parent evenings are intended to provide an opportunity to keep parents informed of academic and behavioural progress of their children and do not provide extended opportunities for in-depth dialogue. However, they can be used to raise and share issues of concern, in a situation where parents do not feel singled out for special attention. Similarly, parent–teacher organisations provide a non-threatening arena in which problems can be aired. While the aims of such bodies are related to matters such as fund raising rather than therapy they can provide a vehicle through which contact can be established and maintained with parents. Many teachers are already aware of the therapeutic potential of the relatively informal parental contact which these situations provide but therapeutic gain does not occur by chance and if such situations are to be fully exploited careful thought and planning must go into the way in which issues are broached and care taken to present a balanced view of the issues involved.

The child's involvement

Children can easily come to suspect some sort of conspiracy if parents and teachers are seen to be working closely without permitting the child any involvement in meetings that take place. Within a systemic framework the child's involvement is highly desirable if not essential and careful thought must be given, whatever model for working with parents is adopted, to the feelings and possible involvement of the child in that process.

Conclusion

In advocating the importance of an approach which conceptualises school-based problems in terms of their context it is important not to underestimate the challenge which this presents to current thinking and practice. Systemic approaches involve a fundamentally different understanding of behaviour problems in schools which deny schools and teachers the possibility of locating problems in behaviour and learning entirely within the individual pupil. While recognising the role which the context of the home may play in the generation of problematic behaviour may not be too difficult for schools, to accept the need to recognise the role which teachers can play in the generation and maintenance of behaviour problems, and the need to face the possibility that intervention must focus sometimes on the teacher rather than the pupil, may be more unpalatable. In the present author's experience teachers and schools do not readily warm to this conceptualisation, and it is important that anyone who attempts to adopt a more contextual approach to working with learning and behavioural difficulties recognises the difficulties that may be encountered, and takes this into account when planning the strategies that might be used and the way in which the approach as a whole might be introduced.

Any attempt to view behaviour or learning problems in context requires teachers to be analytic of their own behaviour and to recognise the perceptions of those with whom they might be in conflict. In this sense approaches such as the ecosystemic approach have, as Tyler (1992) argues, much in common with humanistic approaches to education and counselling which stress the need for teachers to exercise qualities of empathy and foster the development of self-esteem, autonomy and self-direction in their pupils. Such approaches are, thus, far more than strategies for responding to problematic behaviour or under-achievement in that they enrich the teachers' understanding of their interactions with pupils, parents and colleagues which form the core of educational experience. Equally, the emphasis which must be placed on multiple perceptions of events when trying to understand them in their context has important effects for school management structures in that it underlines the value of cooperation among staff and the support that staff can provide for one another in coping with the demands of teaching.

If schools can be encouraged to view problems more in terms of their context, there would thus seem to be great potential benefit not only in terms of the management and amelioration of behaviour and learning difficulties but also in the development of a more generally cooperative and supportive climate within schools and between the schools and parents. Such approaches have the potential to provide teachers and schools with an armoury of techniques with which to respond to a wide range of problems and help make schools more effective for all.

References

Amatea, E.S. (1989) *Brief Strategic Intervention for School Behaviour Problems*. San Francisco: Jossey-Bass.

Brown, D. and Pedder, J. (1979) *Introduction to Psychotherapy*. London: Tavistock.

Burnham, J.B. (1986) *Family Therapy: First Steps Towards a Systemic Approach*. London: Tavistock.

Campion, J. (1985) *The Child in Context: Family Systems Theory in Educational Psychology*. London: Metheun.

Cooper, P. and Upton, G. (1990a) 'An ecosystemic approach to emotional and behaviour in schools'. *Educational Psychology*, 10, 4, pp. 301–323.

Cooper, P. and Upton, G. (1990b) 'Turning conflict into co-operation: an ecosystemic approach to interpersonal conflict and its relevance to pastoral care in schools'. *Pastoral Care in Education*, 8, 4, pp. 10–15.

Dowling, E. and Osborne, D. (1985) *The Family and the School: A Joint Systems Approach to Problems with Children*. London: Routledge.

Hall, N. (1992) 'Psychological and Health Related Problems', in R. Gulliford and G. Upton (eds) *Special Educational Needs*. London: Routledge.

Hamblin, D. (1978) *The Teacher and Counselling*. Oxford: Basil Blackwell.

Molnar, A. and Lindquist, B. (1989) *Changing Problem Behaviour in Schools*. New York: Jossey-Bass.

Power, T. and Bartholomew, K. (1985) 'Getting uncaught in the middle: a case study in family-school system consultation'. *School Psychology Review*, 14, 2, pp. 222–229.

Reynolds, D. (1976) 'The delinquent school', in M. Hammersley and P. Woods (eds) *The Process of Schooling*. Milton Keynes: Open University.

Reynolds, D. (1984) 'The school for vandals: a sociological portrait of the disaffection prone school', in N. Frude and H. Gault (eds) *Disruptive Behaviour in Schools*. Chichester: Wiley.

Rogers, C. (1951) *Client Centred Therapy*. Boston: Houghton Mifflin.

Rutter, M., Maugham, B., Mortimore, P. and Ouston, J. (1979) *Fifteen Thousand Hours: Secondary Schools and their Effects on Children*. London: Open Books.

Sewel, G. (1986) *Coping with Special Needs*. London: Croom Helm.

Tyler, K. (1992) 'The Development of the Ecosystemic Approach as a Humanistic Educational Psychology'. *Educational Psychology*, 12. 1, pp. 15–24.

Upton, G. and Cooper, P. (1990) 'A new perspective on behaviour problems in schools: the ecosystemic approach'. *Maladjustment and Therapeutic Education*, 8, 1, pp. 3–18.

Wheldall, K. and Glynn, T. (1989) *Effective Classroom Learning*. London: Blackwell.

CHAPTER 7

Developing Self-Esteem

Murray White

In this chapter, Murray White describes his work with primary age children in raising self-esteem. In group work, which he calls 'Circle Time', the techniques required in this approach are described. Murray White received an award for the best educational idea in 1990 from the Institute of Social Inventions.

> We create the societies we desire through our schools, but the societies we dream of and proclaim as ideal . . . are very rarely mirrored in the learning institutions to which we entrust our children. (Irwin, 1991)

Imagine if you will a bird's eye view of a school. There is no roof so that you can see into all the classrooms and public areas simultaneously. It is mid-session on a typical day. From your vantage point you observe that all classes are closely involved with the chosen activity, that the children are listening intently or talking animatedly as appropriate, that they are being enthusiastic about the work they are doing, that they are being respectful and tolerant and obviously co-operating with each other. As you continue to watch during the breaks, when there is minimal supervision, you can see that the spirit of friendship and support crosses all age, race and gender barriers and is carried everywhere. The positive atmosphere is all embracing.

What makes some schools more effective than others? There is no one formula for the creation of a successful school; each one has its own unique character. In each case, however, the overall ethos, regardless of size, catchment, buildings, etc., does have one thing in common – the enhancement of the self-esteem of its members. When negative influences and practices have been detected and replaced by positive attitudes and behaviours, an atmosphere of trust and acceptance is created, people's feelings of self-worth are encouraged, their self-esteem is enhanced and children and teachers are keen to be and work together.

How self-esteem affects children's lives

There is increasing evidence of the need for schools to address the issue of self-esteem. The number of children presenting emotional and behavioural difficulties, and consequent exclusions, continues to rise. The pressures on children growing up in a society with such high rates of divorce, unemployment, crime and abuse of all kinds are great indeed. Academic performance and excellence will only rise or be maintained where this is taken into account. Research (Purkey, 1970) now tells us that the correlation between self-esteem and school achievement is as high as that between IQ and school achievement. If the National Curriculum is going to succeed, children have to be able to communicate, decide, risk, be flexible, analyse, evaluate, and get along with others. It is no exaggeration to say that building self-esteem is the best preparation for success at school and in life. There is much that teachers can do to enhance children's self-esteem during the normal day-to-day casual exchanges which happen in every classroom, but it can never be enough. Important as these happenings are, time must be allocated when self-esteem is being actively promoted, as English and mathematics have clear amounts of time given to them. It can be thought of as the fourth R: Reading, Riting, Rithmetic and Relationships. On that aspect alone it merits the time devoted to it.

Developing skills to work in a group is difficult; it does not happen by osmosis. It can be argued that learning to work together is as basic as learning to read and write and should therefore warrant the same amount of teaching time and effort. Professor Maurice Galton is quoted as saying that 'we know you can improve performance by persuading children to co-operate, but few primary teachers are doing that'. (1991)

Circle Time (described fully in White, 1992) is a group process that uses strategies which help children develop skills to understand themselves and to express their individuality. It helps them to appreciate others and the value of friendship, encouraging the individual to be aware of feelings and how to handle them. It assists in how to handle peer pressure and upsets, encouraging co-operation and welcoming new challenges and opportunities to take risks. Decision-making and alternative solutions are brought forward, which promotes self-direction and learning from mistakes.

Strategies which are discussed and learnt during these lessons called Circle Times are then put into practice during other parts of the school day. If a self-esteem policy is to succeed, both parts are essential. It can be compared to a coin; both sides are necessary to make it complete. Where this has taken place, teachers have noticed 'a more pleasant atmosphere in the classroom', a unifying influence in the class' and 'much interactive, collaborative, and corroborative behaviour'. One teacher wrote that:

> After two years involvement with Circle Time, my school seems to be far more settled. There are far fewer instances of
> (a) confrontations of an unpleasant nature between children;
> (b) children 'in trouble' standing outside the Head's Office;
> (c) vandalism, aggression and complaints from parents;
>   and far more instances of
> (a) children showing responsibility for their actions;
> (b) teachers emphasising the positive;
> (c) co-operation and help from parents and children in the running of the school.
>
> This may be a huge coincidence... but I think not. (White, 1990)

When children are in a school where relationship skills are given time and attention, the impact on their lives is far reaching. Not only do these skills increase their immediate ability to communicate well, they give a real bonus in their adult lives. During a visit to the United States I was told that the National Labor Board had conducted a large survey (1988) to find out why people got the sack. It discovered that the majority of employers were quite satisfied with the technical skills their employees brought to their jobs, but when they came in contact with others, whether it was the employers themselves, their peers, or if the post required it, with the public, then they were less than satisfactory. Seventy per cent of employees in the survey were dismissed for this reason.

A teacher who recognised the importance of these skills and how Circle Time would help wrote:

Circle Time has resulted in my being far less eager to sort organisation out in my classroom as I believe the children are quite capable of talking through and tackling these problems themselves. This in turn gives them a greater sense of independence and responsibility. As they have more say in how the classroom is run they look after things better and take more pride in its appearance and running.

Another said:

I believe the children find Circle Time a valuable and meaningful part of the school day. They want to work harder and co-operate with others because they feel of worth themselves.

When I started Circle Time about five years ago, my aim was to help the children in the school to learn readily and behave well. From my observation it had become apparent to me, and for the reasons already stated, that many were finding these two objectives increasingly difficult. I could see that many problems seemed to persist regardless of the efforts of both children and adults. It was obvious that some of the children often appeared less able than they really were and that much of the anti-social behaviour, both passive and aggressive, originated in an underlying lack of self-confidence. This was having a domino effect so that increasing numbers of children were being influenced in a negative way and staff energies and skills were being tested to the limit.

I decided that the school curriculum needed to take more account of affective education, as opposed to the cognitive, intellectual approach. Emphasis on the latter was failing the children and a better balance needed to be achieved. Affective education, through Circle Time, would help children think more positively about themselves, give them greater opportunities to be more responsible for themselves, and encourage and give them skills to make better and wiser decisions. The intention was to go beyond helping children to feel good about themselves, important as that is. I certainly agree with Purkey (1970) when he says that 'students who feel good about themselves and their abilities are the ones most likely to succeed' but self-esteem is wider than that.

Self-esteem is the respect and value of the self. It is the concept that there is real importance in what we do, think, feel, and believe. Self-esteem is the knowledge that we do make a difference, positive or negative, that we have an effect on others and the environment, that we are in charge of our own lives. Self-esteem is the knowledge that nothing is stagnant, that everything changes, and that we are strong enough and valuable enough to deal with the changes. High self-esteem is the belief in ourselves that we have the power to choose and the confidence to make decisions about what we do in our lives.

Children with low self-esteem do not have these thoughts about themselves and walk into school every day believing themselves to be unloved, unwanted and rejected, feeling discouraged, powerless, inadequate and incompetent. These ideas are demonstrated by the things that say and do. They make comments such as 'I hate it', 'There's never anything to do', 'This is stupid', 'No-one plays with me', 'It's his fault'. They can be seen showing off inappropriately, bullying and bragging, and constantly blaming others or they are obviously reluctant to express opinions, unwilling to take responsibility, or unwilling to try anything new. They are sometimes rude and lack compassion; others may be fearful and timid. These behaviours are clearly the product of low self-esteem and keep children trapped in a downward spiral of failure and despair. In order to provide them with an opportunity to break this cycle of failure it is essential that teachers have the commitment, learn the skills, and find the time to be involved with this level of the children's lives. In my experience the rewards are immense.

Developing self-esteem through Circle Time

Circle Time sets out to provide a setting where children will feel safe and supported and be secure enough to try out different ways of behaving – a real learning laboratory. It quickly finds favour with the children. Of the hundreds of children that I know who have participated in Circle Time, and apart from an initial reluctance from a very small number, they have all taken part with great enthusiasm. Their comments are witness to that, and young as some of them are, they are very perceptive as to what it is all about: 'It gives you a chance to share your feelings', 'You get to trust people more'. The clarity with which individual differences are accepted and valued are so appreciated: 'It is very good in the way everyone gets a chance to speak and everyone listens to you.' 'I think it helps us as a class because everyone sees others points of view.' 'It helps us not to be shy and to say what we think.'

Being helped to grow emotionally and to enhance your self-esteem is a very popular activity. Statements like these are common: 'Circle Time is a good experience for us children.' 'Circle Time is the best part of the day.' 'Everyone enjoys Circle Time because it wakes us up a bit and helps us to relax before a long day at school; also we get a good laugh out of it. I will miss Circle Time when I go to secondary school because it's worth coming to school for!' I once read that Socrates would listen outside the doors of the classrooms of his school and if he did not hear laughter within five minutes he would go in to see what was wrong. Circle Time creates a climate where children can be truly spontaneous, and even though serious issues are dealt with, they will relax, sometimes laugh, certainly learn and undoubtedly flourish. As one child wrote: 'I realised there was nothing to be frightened of because we all shared each other's problems.'

Circle Times are often called Magic Circles because of the transformational effects on the participants. I believe the term Circle Time was first used by others when bringing small groups of children together in a circle for social skills training. If resources allow, I can see the advantages of working with a small number at certain times, such as when there are very particular difficulties to be tackled, but generally I think it is so much better to have the whole class together. Only then will trust and security be established and the group dynamic operate well.

The circle shape is very important. Jung (Jaffé, 1978) referred to it as a symbol of wholeness and many cultures and societies have always used it, for example, King Arthur and the Round Table. It represents, among other things, equality, mutual respect, participation, involvement in decision making. In Circle Time there is a heightened awareness of these compared to when the usual organisation in the room is operating, and the children welcome and very readily accept the opportunities for these experiences that it presents. A teacher wrote of one boy that:

> He seemed to be on another planet when doing 'normal' class work, but really comes alive and makes some interesting and intelligent comments in Circle Time. In fact, I feel now that he is far more intelligent than ordinary class work shows. My aim now is to motivate and energise him into activity. Without Circle Time I would have written him off as Special Needs as he has two gears – dead slow and stop!

As my own experience of Circle Time has increased and my research into self-esteem has progressed I have been able to build a structure for Circle Time which I believe includes the best practices available to promote self-esteem. I see this structure as three interlocking wheels, incorporating the theory of self-esteem, the activities which enhance it, and the process which develops while it is happening (see Figure 7.1).

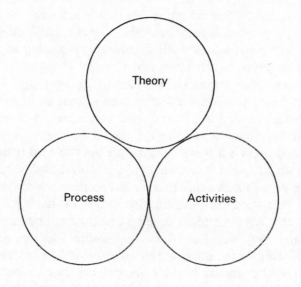

Figure 7.1   The structure of circle time

The components of self-esteem

It was Maslow, through his Hierarchy of Needs, who drew attention to the importance of a feeling of security in everyone's life. It was he who said 'Only a child who feels safe dares to grow forward healthily. His safety needs must be gratified' (Maslow, 1968). If we have our need for stability and structure met, it gives a sense of security that we are grounded somewhere. Research is pointing clearly to the impact on children's sense of security of divorce, unemployment – a UNICEF report (1990) said that children in this country bore the brunt of economic disadvantage in the 1980s – and abuse in all its forms. Witnessing the results of drugs, violence and crime, all increasing, strains security to its limits. Sir Michael Rutter, Professor of Child Psychiatry at the University of London, is quoted as saying 'For children in an unrewarding environment, good experiences at school can make quite a big difference. They can offer experiences which help certain children and are potentially beneficial to all' (Robins, 1992). I maintain the Circle Time is an ideal forum to provide those good experiences.

Security is the pivot of the framework. The second basic ingredient necessary for the growth of self-esteem is a sense of identity. In order to have self-esteem each of us needs to feel special. We cannot afford to feel like a nonentity, like someone who does not matter. Children – and adults – need to feel recognised as individuals and that they are worthwhile people whose ideas are valued by others. With this sense of identity will come a lot of self-knowledge, including an accurate description in terms of attributes and physical characteristics and a keen awareness of emotions and the part they play in life. As well as discovering their uniqueness, children need a sense of belonging. We all need to feel needed and loved, and connected to other human beings. The way adolescents are influenced by their peers in their behaviour and dress is a powerful example but the need remains with us throughout life, and if we want to maintain a high level of self-esteem then we will make sure that we have a network of people who will satisfy that need. Self-esteem also hinges on having a sense of purpose in life. When children develop one they will be motivated to set goals and they will learn how to consider options and make choices. The role of the adult at this stage is vital to ensure that the goals are realistic and achievable. A balance has to be arranged between security and risk, and when it is attained success will generate more success. This in turn will promote a sense of competence, which gives children the belief that they have the power to succeed in the things they regard as important and valuable. With this sense they will be aware of their strengths and proud of them. When children experience success and express it as clearly as Christine, aged ten, did when she said to a student on practice 'I'm really proud of my model. It's a nice feeling to feel proud, isn't it?' then I know they will be able to deal effectively and creatively with all life situations.

Some people ask if the time spent in Circle Time can be justified for those children who already have good self-esteem. No one can ever have too much self-esteem. It always needs maintenance and can be further enhanced. It can be compared to physical health. We never say we have more than we want and what we have we need to maintain and cherish and improve upon if possible. Branden (1987) says that all problems, apart from those that are biological in origin, are traceable to low self-esteem. With a high sense of esteem every problem, any challenge, will be easier to solve; or if it can't be solved, it will be possible to handle it with greater poise and strength; that argument alone makes it a worthwhile experience for every child. It gives them valuable opportunities to discover full potential and to embrace no limit living.

Special Days raise self-esteem

The many activities which are used in Circle Time are fully described elsewhere (White, 1992), but one is worth a particular mention, because, whereas all the others can be varied and mixed up and put in from time to time, this one should be done at every Circle Time, first, because the effect in raising self-esteem is so apparent and, second, because it is a winner with the children: 'I think Special Days are good for us because it makes us want to come to school more and enjoy what we are learning at the same time.'

The Special Day procedure is based on a formula aiming to promote a combination of a sense of security, identity and belonging at the same time. Its beginning always generates a lot of excitement. This is because the children know that one of them is to be selected to have a Special Day – this is just one reason why it's good to begin the day with Circle Time although some teachers do it successfully at other times for organisational reasons. The child must be selected in a random way so there is an element of surprise and selection: it must be seen to be fair. The easiest is to pick names out of a hat but there are more imaginative ways. Everyone knows he or she will get a turn eventually: 'Special Days are all right because everyone gets a turn. I haven't been chosen yet but I'm looking forward to the day.'

There are many reasons why Circle Time should happen every day, despite pressures on the timetable. Apart from the opportunities for more personal growth each time it's done, if it starts each day it is more likely that the children will use it to discharge any stress that has been brought to school, that they will re-connect to the security of the circle and their friends and there will be less disruption and more work done during the rest of the day. The over-riding reason for the children, however, is probably because it will bring their turn to have a Special Day that much closer. If Circle Time occurs every day, then it means that every child in an average size class will have two Special Days a term, six a year. This is because the procedure is repeated once everyone has had a turn, using a different means of selection. If ever there was an activity which is universally popular and which benefits everyone then this is it.

One key way to get children to think positively about themselves is to get them to make positive statements to others. It has been shown quite clearly that one of the most effective ways of enhancing children's self-esteem is to get them to praise others. One study (Brady, 1978) showed improved scores for *all* children who took part. This Special Day procedure is an excellent vehicle for this to take place. When the child is selected, he or she is invited to sit in the middle of the circle. After the presentation of a badge which can be worn all day as a reminder to the rest of the class and for identification purposes with the rest of the school, the compliments can begin. All the children are invited to take turns to say things to this child which *they think he or she would like to hear*. All remarks should be prefaced by words such as 'I like...', to indicate that it is the speaker's opinion. For example, if the child is told that the speaker thinks he is clever or good-looking and that conflicts with a low estimate of himself it cannot be subconsciously rejected. That is most important otherwise a child with low self-esteem is unable to accept these statements. Obviously sincerity is the keynote: no-one is forced to say anything they do not mean. A sensitive teacher can soon encourage the compliments to flow and even if the youngest children can only say they like the colour of the selected child's socks it's a beginning and things soon progress. The ordinary civilities are missing in so many children's lives today and even 'Good morning, it's good to see you' is valuable. Lists of positive qualities can be displayed nearby to act as a reminder of compliments to consider. Things can always be found to be said to even the most unpopular child; children begin to look for the positive qualities which everyone has.

For many this is a new experience; society is awash with negativity and lots of children are immersed in it. In their homes, children often hear many more negative statements than positive ones. In the book *School Matters* (Mortimore, 1988), a study of fifty London junior schools, observers noted that teachers spent only one per cent of their time giving praise. Someone else has calculated that children can expect to hear 15,000 negative statements in a school year, amounting to sixty days in a school career when nothing else is heard! Children who speak civilly to each other in the classroom are less likely to be aggressive to each other in the playground and elsewhere. Its effects on the reduction of bullying are substantial as are other strategies employed in Circle Time. Good self-esteem will certainly lessen a child's need to bully. People who get negative attention don't think they can get positive attention or compliments. Bullies and trouble makers are making signals that they need some positive attention and when they get it in Circle Time – and it's here where you see how influential peers are – then the results can be dramatic. One session like this can be worth ten one-to-one sessions with an adult. Equally important is that the potential victim is strengthened in Circle Time.

107

Children move from each end of the passive–aggressive continuum and learn how to assert themselves in win–win situations. The benefits even extend to onlookers as they will certainly be inclined to intervene in a positive way in a bullying situation. High self-esteem encourages social responsibility; another result is less graffiti and vandalism.

The remarks made to the selected child should be recorded in some way – we made a special certificate – and handed to the child to keep. No-one can remember them all when faced with a barrage but it is good to think of what was said later on. For many children it is an experience of a lifetime and it is often moving to witness. The children listen with quiet pleasure. Some make real discoveries. One 11 year old boy was told by others that they admired his ability to keep calm when faced with aggression. The next day the group was discussing 'feeling' words and he suggested 'surprised'. When asked to elaborate he said he had been surprised to find out how much he was liked. He joined in discussions much more confidently after that. Sometimes the repercussions go beyond the classroom. One teacher notes: 'Parents are coming to find out what is happening in the class to make the children so keen to get there.' Another says 'Parents are asking for confirmation that the other children really did say all these things about their child and subsequently framing their Special Day certificates. It is always interesting to ask the children which comments mean most to them. 'You are nice to be with' is always a favourite and often new liaisons begin or old ones are revived because of these public declarations.

The child is then asked to name one thing about himself about which he is pleased. It often causes difficulty and here we see the measure of low self-esteem. One capable girl hesitated for some while before saying 'I am good at maths' and then adding in a whisper 'sometimes'. We do a great disservice to our children if we do not teach them the difference between boasting and bragging and being proud of their achievements. One registers low, the other high self-esteem, and they need to be able to recognise this. The ceremony, which doesn't actually take long, has several other important components. Feeling secure, the child may be invited to try out some new behaviour today, a small risk of some kind, just to see how it feels. If it shows benefits it can be adopted, if not discarded. The withdrawn child will often be more adventurous on these days, the more boisterous may try some quieter activities. The advantages of giving feedback in a safe situation can be clearly identified.

The child can claim special privileges for the day. The badge is the passport to being able to do 'anything reasonable'. The privileges vary from school to school. If equipment is short then this child has first turn; if he wants to sit on a chair at the front at assembly then he can do so; if he wants tea or coffee from the staffroom at break he may have it; if he wants to depart from the normal timetabled activity, perhaps with a friend, he may do so, provided the work is done at some other time. These privileges are not abused. Another thing that the child can do is to choose the game which is normally played at this point. It is selected from a list of games which will promote self-esteem in some way. It doesn't take long, is an energiser for the beginning of the day and is great fun.

If the theory is correct and the activities work, then the third wheel will turn and in the process the children:

- will come to understand themselves and be able to express their own individuality;
- will be able to appreciate others and the value of friendship;
- will become aware of feelings and handle them in a healthy way;
- will be able to resist peer pressure and handle upsets; and
- will co-operate and share.

From there they:

- will be ready to welcome new challenges and the opportunities to take risks;
- will be able to look for alternative solutions, make decisions and learn from mistakes;
- will cope with any changes and difficulties; and
- will appreciate that life is a special occasion and they will rise to it!

The Circle Time network

As a result of the publication of an article I wrote about my early experiences in Circle Times, many teachers have adopted this way of working with their children and lots have given me valuable feedback. This was increased further when, on secondment, I was able to lead Circle Time in other schools and get the reactions of the staff. Many benefits were identified, as well as responsible behaviour and good co-operation. Language proficiency was specially highlighted:

> One of my early observations was how quickly the children's speech

improved. One word became ten as they experimented with words and found a variety of ways in which they could be used.

Numerous aspects of the National Curriculum can be covered by work in Circle Time. There is stress on children being able to listen to each other, voice an opinion and sustain an argument. Circle Time is ideal for getting children into small groups to discuss issues and report back to the group as a whole. In Circle Time children can take part as speakers and listeners with increased confidence and be actively encouraged to comment constructively. Ideas and information are re-evaluated and logical argument can be practised. By giving the children something to talk about which they know, they become active participants in their own learning. They are able to see it is their thoughts and knowledge which are being valued and sought after, that they are a valuable resource.

One person was kind enough to write and say: 'Congratulations on pioneering something truly relevant to the development of young people.' However I think the summing up is best left to a sturdy, wide-eyed eight year old who wrote: 'Circle Time is very, very, very good.'

References

Brady, P. J. *et al*. (1978) 'Predicting Student Self Concept, Anxiety and Responsibility from Self-Evaluation and Self Praise', *Psychology in Schools*, Vol. 15.
Branden, N. (1987) *How To Raise Your Self-Esteem*. New York: Bantam Books.
Irwin, C. (1991) *Education and the Development of Social Integration in Divided Societies*. Council For Integrated Education, Northern Ireland.
Galton, M. (November, 1991) *Times Educational Supplement*.
Jaffé, A. (1978) *Man and His Symbols, edited Carl Jung*. London: Picador.
Maslow, A. (1968) *Toward A Psychology Of Being*. New York: Van Nostrand Reinhold.
Mortimore, P. *et al*. (1988) *School Matters, The Junior Years*. Somerset: Open Book Publishing Ltd.
Purkey, W. (1970) *Self Concept and School Achievement*. New York: Prentice Hall.
Robins, L. N. and Rutter, M. (1992) *Straight and Devious Pathways from Childhood to Adulthood*. Cambridge University Press.
White, M. (1990) *Magic Circles – The Benefits of Circle Time*. Cambridge: Esteem Workshops.
White, M. (1992) *Self-Esteem – Its Meaning And Value In Schools*. Cambridge: Daniels Publishing.

CHAPTER 8

Peer Support Groups and Whole School Development

Charles Mead and Paul Timmins

Charles Mead and Paul Timmins address the issues surrounding stress in the work place – this being the school. They identify the use of Peer Support Groups to reduce it. They offer practical approaches which institutions may use to set up these groups. This chapter clearly deals with the individual needs of the educator.

> 'Work, is, by its very nature, about violence – to the spirit as well as the body. It is about ulcers as well as accidents, about shouting matches as well as fistfights, about nervous breakdowns as well as kicking the dog around. It is above all (or beneath all) about daily humiliations. To survive the day is triumph enough for the walking wounded among the great many of us.' (Allington and Cooper *et al.*, 1989, p. 387)

Introduction

These sentiments confront us with the raw experience of work, and remind us of its effects on our lives. Our contention is that schools possess the resources to identify individual and organisationally related sources of stress and the ability to reduce these. We suggest that Peer Support Groups (PSGs) provide a basis for reducing the pressures of school life, and offer a basis for individual and institutional (school) development. Our notion of this type of group is that it should form a focus for its work through negotiation with senior staff in school, based on the institution's needs, and that through collaborative working, group members will develop both professionally and personally, and through their negotiated brief also help in the overall development of the host institution.

We develop our argument by reviewing findings relating to the experience of stress in school settings, and the links between stress and school organisation and practice. This is followed by an examination of the processes and benefits associated with Support Groups (SGs) and PSGs, and the anthropological and psychological evidence for the universality, effectiveness and adaptive nature of co-operative behaviour in groups. There then follows a section which focuses on the formation of a PSG, as a working group. This chapter concludes with a highly practical section describing structures and processes which institutions might use to convene and maintain PSGs, in the light of staff and organisational need.

Much of the research described in this chapter is a product of the positivist tradition of empirical research (Cohen and Manion, 1989). Whilst we are happy to use these findings to help describe the benefits of PSGs, we are less happy with the methodological framework used and its ability to provide institutions with a means of achieving proper ownership of initiatives, and practical and meaningful methods of evaluating their effectiveness. To fill this methodological gap, we drew heavily on the principles and processes reflected in Collaborative Action Research, for example Oja and Smulyan (1989), the New Paradigm (Reason and Rowan, 1981; Reason, 1988) and Conversational approaches (Thomas and Harri-Augstein, 1985; Harri-Augstein and Thomas, 1991). These combine to make a practical contribution to the reflective processes of planning action, action and review.

Teacher stress, stress reduction and whole school development

Research on the causes and effects of stress in the teaching profession grew exponentially in the 1980s (Kyriacou and Sutcliffe, 1978; Dunham, 1984; AMMA, 1986; Cox et al., 1988; Johnstone, 1989; Rees, 1989). Teachers consistently identified problem pupils and indiscipline, lack of support, failings in leadership, poor working conditions (both physical and psychological), lack of communication, poor pay, role ambiguity, role conflict and conflict in relationships, as stressors (AMMA, 1986; Rees, 1989). Borg and Riding (1991) described studies which indicated that between 19 and 30 per cent of teachers reported being very or extremely stressed by their work. Definitions of stress recognise the uniqueness of personal experience and response and associate these with discomfort and perceived threat to self-esteem. High and persistent levels of stress are associated with 'burn out', symptoms being increased absenteeism, lack of directional focus, high levels of complaining, lack of communication, trust and positive feedback (Rees, 1989).

Many of the stressors described above would appear to be amenable to some measure of reduction through PSG type initiatives; indeed, evidence we present below suggests that group membership may reduce teachers' feelings of alienation and increase feelings of control over work. Gray and Freeman (1987) and ESAC (1990) suggest that this type of support may play a part in stress management and reduction.

As the findings above imply, the experience of stress is likely to depend upon personal perception, interacting with the unwitting (one hopes) effects of school organisation, procedure and practice. Thus schools need to research the effects on staff and promote the development of PSGs in a systematic manner. Research of this type, as part of general school development, is encouraged by a variety of approaches relying on the concept of the working group, for example, GRIDS (1988) and Hargreaves et al. (1990). Other approaches, such as those described in the introduction above, and more particularly, the System Supplied Information (Myers et al., 1989), MAPPER (Myers and Cherry, 1990) and Self-Organised Learning (Harri-Augstein and Thomas, 1991; Timmins and Dunkley, 1990), directly address the harmonisation of individual and institutional needs. As implied above, in the latter part of this chapter, we focus on processes which might be used by such groups (PSGs) to organise their work and promote a feeling of well-being, both within the group and at its interface with the wider school organisation.

The universality of co-operative behaviour and the benefits of social support

Fiske (1991) writes that 'the axiom of the primacy of selfish individualism is contradicted by numerous cross-cultural studies and historical analyses and by examination of ethnographic evidence from a wide variety of cultures' (p. 176) and 'what the ethnographic evidence shows is that prosocial behaviour is universal, helping is the mode and altruism is very common' (p. 177). Argyle (1991), in an extensive study of the roots of co-operation in society, argues that co-operative behaviour is of evolutionary value and notes that such behaviour needs to be learned, encouraged and maintained, through appropriate social structures. (We view PSGs as examples of co-operative behaviour.) Further, he provides support for the rather intriguing notion that engaging in co-operative behaviour is linked with the release of brain chemicals associated with pleasant mood states, and evidence of the superiority of co-operative group problem solving over more individualised forms.

Caplan (1976) provides an extensive account of the use of groups for therapeutic purposes. These are widely referred to as Support Groups (SGs) and focus largely on the personal emotional needs of participating members, usually being led by skilled, professional facilitators. Examples include groups for the bereaved, step-parents, alcoholics, and we would also include encounter and therapy groups aimed at developing the 'whole person'. Although it is our intention to promote the idea of self-managed groups, with a predominantly institutional, task-related focus, we feel it is worth describing research on the benefits of facilitating groups, as some features of the observed effects and processes appear relevant to our work on PSGs.

Wills (1991) isolated features of SG membership perceived to be linked with improved ability to cope with life-stressors; these included the sharing of information, guidance and advice, social companion-ship and perhaps most significantly a sense of emotional support. This latter factor is reliably identified across a number of studies, as a contributory factor in the maintenance of self-esteem, which stems from activities involving self-disclosure and a sense of valued social contact. Wills also notes a degree of commonality between these findings and factors thought to be determinants of adjustment in psychotherapy research. He also found evidence one might expect: that there is a reduced incidence of mortality where individuals have high levels of social ties defined in terms of marriage, contacts with friends and relatives, and church and group membership.

Peer support groups: examples and benefits

Examples of these groups are found more readily in the American education literature where the term seems to have originated. Tracking down evaluated examples of PSGs in the UK has proved more difficult, possibly because of a lack of a commonly shared descriptor. (We would expect UK studies to fall under a variety of headings, for instance, the GRIDS (1988) approach may have stimulated many projects, though we doubt whether they will have been evaluated from a Peer Support perspective.)

Zins *et al.* (1988) describe the use of PSGs to enhance the professional skills and knowledge of School Psychologists. Santora (1988) involved staff in an English Department in the mutually beneficial sharing of English teaching skills. Paquette (1987) used 'Collegial Support' groups, comprising a mixture of subject specialists and school managers, to provide a climate to support professional development.

In each of these applications the skills necessary for effective group facilitation and leadership were available in the institutions involved. Some PSG applications demand higher order group management skills. Thies-Sprinthall and Gerler (1990) describe a counsellor led support group for probationary teachers. The need for facilitation was justified in terms of the stressful nature of this first year of teaching. Hanko (1985) facilitated groups for teachers which focused on the discussion of pupils whose behaviour was described as disturbed and disturbing, and her work is further developed and reported by Stringer *et al.* (1992). Kearney and Turner (1987) worked with a group of headteachers to help identify and deal with sources of stress.

Hanko's teachers reported increased confidence as a result of discovering that they shared similar problems and difficulties. They also valued the suggestions and perspectives of others in terms of learning how to work with pupils over time, rather than expecting quick-fix strategies. There was also evidence that some teachers achieved insight into the relationship between their needs and responses to pupil behaviour. Furthermore, heads of participating schools commented on the increased professionalism of staffroom discussion; many heads requested groups of their own.

Over time, Thies-Sprinthall's group experienced a reduction in perceived stress, tension, and feelings of isolation, with an increased tendency to see difficulties as a challenge, and to respond by attempting to improve professional competence. Feelings of increased professional competence and group morale were also reported in the studies carried out by Zins and Santora.

A comparison of SGs and PSGs: some implications for the development of PSGs in schools

Caplan (1976) encourages professions to:

> ... learn to appreciate the fortifying potential of the natural person-to-person supports in the population and to find ways of working with them through some form of partnership that fosters non-professional groups and organisations ... [in order] ... to augment the capacity of individuals to master their environments in mentally healthy ways, particularly individuals made vulnerable because they are involved in acute crises, life transitions, or chronic privations. (pp. 19–20)

In this statement, and Argyle (1991) and Fiske (1991), we see a clear implication for schools that their organisational structures should reinforce natural forms of social support. Caplan's approach suggests a need for a skilled group leader; more recently Nichols and Jenkinson (1991) see SGs as being led successfully on a peer-basis, using the natural group process (self-disclosure, mutual support and understanding, reflecting on feelings and confronting difficult issues) as a basis for providing support and enhancing professional skills. Their description of SG work appears to be best suited to a stress management approach based largely on the group processing of feelings about work, with an expectation that individual group members will subsequently be better equipped to cope with work related tasks.

Our interpretation of the function of the PSG encompasses this notion of support which is seen to emanate from high quality interpersonal communication within the group, but to this we add the potential for the group to work collaboratively with an additional task-oriented focus, a possibility not clearly evident in the work of Caplan (1976) and Nichols and Jenkinson (1991). By task-oriented, we mean a focus or purpose agreed with the group and possibly further refined through negotiation with school managers, this being related to a whole school development issue or the professional development of PSG members. We see PSG developed plans and actions relating to these purposes as being achieved through cycles of reflection and action which would include group managed reviews of two major aspects of PSG life – the quality of the support function of the group for its members and the extent to which the task orientation of the group is effectively pursued.

These levels of processing provide a basis for self-managed professional development and promote the development of a learning culture within the group, thus contributing to a positive school ethos and improved, individual professional practice. Within our approach to PSGs there is also a strong assumption that the processes we describe to guide their establishment and maintenance will result in greater feelings of ownership and personal competence amongst group members in relation to PSG focus and perhaps beyond. For us, these benefits derive from the collaborative formulation of purposes and associated action, and the evaluation of outcomes achieved by the PSG.

In the following sections, we provide practically based elaborations of these themes, these being heavily influenced by Harri-Augstein and Thomas's (1991) theory of Self-Organised Learning. Our intention is to provide the reader with a framework for developing PSGs in their own institutions to provide both support for staff and a basis for institutional development.

Groups: problems, leadership and facilitation

For those with a measure of curiosity about the origins of tensions we observe and sometimes create in groups, psychodynamic approaches to psychology provide some fascinating insights and an interpretive framework to help work out what might be going on. They identify a particular phenomenon, termed transference, thought to hinder group development. Here, a group member's behaviour (with unconscious roots in infancy and unresolved problems with parent figures) leads to difficulties in coping with the content of group discussions, or the role of the group leader, and results in a particularly difficult group dynamic requiring skilled interpretation and intervention. See for example, Skynner's (1989) account of a support group for the staff of an inner city secondary school, which includes descriptions of such dynamics and his attempts to understand and change these; Klein (1979) provides a more detailed consideration of the part played by transference in group life.

Other perspectives on group facilitation and the causes of difficulties in groups, particularly those involving some degree of exploration of the emotional and personal lives of group members, can be found in Nelson-Jones (1991), Killilea (1976), Collins and Bruce (1984), Nichols and Jenkinson (1991), Hanko (1985) and Stringer et al. (1992). Approaches to working with groups described in these sources are more accessible to the teacher-practitioner than methods described in the psychodynamic literature, which require specialist training.

The PSG as a working group

The preceding sections have provided the theoretical basis for our contention that PSGs may fulfil a useful role in reducing teacher stress and thus improving overall school performance. This part of the chapter examines the role of a working group within a school setting. We look at the advantages and disadvantages of working as a group and suggest an approach to team building that should help avoid the pitfalls of group work and produce an effective vehicle for both change and personal learning.

We also suggest that the way a PSG is organised and facilitated may either reinforce or ameliorate any problems or pressures felt by staff in schools. The object of a PSG is to provide an antidote to the potentially morale-sapping experience of some aspects of school life through a coherent and unifying approach, where staff have some control, and ownership of, the means of developing such a project.

The function of a PSG

A Peer Support Group (PSG) is a working group within an organisation and as such could become a basic part of a teacher's professional life. The PSG could become the means for collaboration between staff on a range of issues outlined later. Its basic function would be to allow staff to communicate concerns of an individual or organisational nature, and then attempt to tackle these concerns.

There is evidence that some work groups do not function well (Newton and Levinson, 1973) in that they:

- do little to achieve the tasks for which they were created; and
- do not manage to produce constructive or collaborative behaviour amongst their members.

This would inevitably produce a lack of satisfaction in teachers and a less than effective service to pupils and the school as a whole.

To establish a successful PSG it is therefore essential to have an awareness of how a working group functions. The desire for effective interaction between teachers will not be enough for PSGs to sustain themselves. Any PSG, or PSG facilitator, needs to be aware of the way in which groups may be set up and managed in order to develop a PSG, and for it to function effectively.

One function of a PSG might be an attempt to reduce stress in staff, so that they may be better teachers. There is a danger though that a PSG that is seen to fail could produce more stress. Schools are becoming large, competitive organisations, having to co-ordinate an increasingly large number of activities. It is no wonder that teachers feel the ground move under their feet. Central and local government pressures have created uncertainty, complexity and unpredictability for teachers. If feelings of, say, superficiality, segmentation and isolation are caused by the changing role of schools, then any group set up to help teachers overcome these feelings should be aware of what they are potentially dealing with, and so develop their PSGs accordingly.

Personal responses to group work

Teachers are required to be instructors, advisers, resource-finders and general 'fixers', but the way in which their work is organised and discussed rarely allows them to recognise each other as real people with feelings. Their emotional response to their work comes with the job, but it is because they cannot entirely look to their clients for support that they need to develop supportive frameworks for themselves at work.

It follows that there is an apparent need for any PSG to be supportive of staff in the way that it functions, not just in the tasks it sets itself (Dockar-Drysdale, 1973). For example, a PSG that ignores the stress factors inherent in a school could lead to a climate where staff deny their anxiety and uncertainty about concerns they have. Instead of a supportive structure where stress can be recognised, worked on and contained, the PSG sustains the stress, or worsens it, by ignoring it.

Addressing staff concerns within a PSG

One of the difficulties a newly established PSG might face, especially where strong feelings are likely to be expressed, is the lack of a model to structure and so make sense of those feelings. Within the PSG, and the staff it may attempt to support, this may lead to teachers becoming suspicious of one another, and so add the stress of conflict with colleagues to the already stressful situation of working with clients.

To avoid these pitfalls any PSG would need to be based on the following beliefs:

● a recognition that all staff work for the same school and towards the same ends;

- that it is in the best interests of the school for staff to care for each other's professional work;
- that it is through sharing experiences, both positive and negative, that support can be given;
- that by working together a solution can be found to individual and organisational concerns.

Furthermore, the super-ordinate principles of the PSG, its purpose and role, must be clearly established before the task-based activities of tackling specific concerns and implementing strategies for change are initiated.

If the concerns of PSG members (or staff with concerns) are tackled, then norms develop about what is, and is not, permissible to discuss or feel within the group. It is essential that the creation of such norms are compatible with the PSG as a force for change with the school.

Further perspectives on the causes of difficulties in groups and on group facilitation, particularly those involving some degree of exploration of the emotional and personal lives of group members, can be found in Nelson-Jones (1991), Killilea (1976), Collins and Bruce (1984), Nichols and Jenkinson (1991) and Hanko (1985).

Approaches to working with groups described in these sources are more accessible to the teacher-practitioner than methods described in the psychodynamic literature, which require specialist training (Skynner, 1989; Klein, 1979).

The impact of change strategies through PSG development

We do not suggest that a PSG is a radical force. That may prove threatening to staff and school. We suggest, though, that a PSG needs to be aware of its potential role and be further aware of an individual's or organisation's resistance to change (Schon, 1971). At its best a PSG can encourage change in the behaviour of staff in order to elicit change in the behaviour of pupils. To be successful, however, there must be a recognition of the impact of change strategies in organisational settings, in particular that:

- any process of reform must expect and encourage some form of conflict; usually internally and individually, but on occasions also on an organisational scale;
- effective change strategies respect the different levels of experience of teachers, so that they may organise their own agenda for change in a comfortable way;

● there must be enough time and support given to PSG members and individual staff to accommodate any suggested change so that they can give their own meanings to their experiences.

It is likely that if a PSG planned task is implemented impatiently any expected change is unlikely to occur and, worse, that unanticipated and undesirable changes may result.

The teambuilding approach to establishing a PSG

A way of ensuring a successful PSG is through a teambuilding approach. In practical terms this means that a PSG should successfully tackle a concern as soon as possible after its formation in order to show its worth. By implication it should therefore choose a 'do-able' task. The process of task identification and related action enhances the teambuilding process. It is widely used organisational development strategy and is best described as a cyclical process where, after each cycle, the group is able to review its work, learn and plan the next cycle more effectively. This can be represented as Figure 8.1. The process will be refined in the next section on establishing a PSG. The outcomes for groups working in this way are broadly seen as valuable for the individual member, the PSG and the school as a whole. All three could become better at:

● spotting problems;
● learning new strategies to cope with problems;
● recognising that change can be positive;
● developing more positive attitudes towards colleagues.

PSG/staff with concern
(which may relate to own work or organisational need)

Collection of information by PSG/staff on particular concerns

Diagnosing the problem presented by PSG/staff to identify concerns

Feeding this information to the PSG, if a staff concern

PSG discuss the information and concerns

An Action Plan is drawn up

Action is taken

The outcomes of the action are recorded

PSG reviews the process

Figure 8.1 The cyclical process

It is important to recognise that PSG events on their own will be relatively ineffectual in changing a whole school. A PSG should not be a threat to management, nor a flagship for individual staff wanting change within a whole-school approach. To work well and gain the trust of colleagues, a PSG needs to be supportive of the whole school and be integrated within its present structure. The most effective role of a PSG is in being a vehicle for addressing staff concerns about their own work, or that of the school, in a task-based way.

However, the emphasis on a PSG being a vehicle for personal learning and team building is a result of the need for individuals to make sense of their environment and the organisational structures in which they work. Top-down bureaucracies are poor learning systems (Argyris and Schon, 1987) so individuals need to have the opportunity to develop a clear understanding of their role in school, on both a personal and professional level. An effective way of doing this is to provide a framework where staff can learn for themselves how best to cope, especially by developing clear ways of communicating with each other about their needs and their perceptions of the needs of their school.

A PSG has the capacity to develop along these lines. To do so it needs to be open and democratic in structure, avoiding hierarchical divisions, where its members are recruited on the basis of competence and the group can negotiate its own role within the school.

One of the main functions of a PSG will be to encourage staff to critically review their own work roles in a positive and supportive way, harnessing rather than undermining the personal and emotional response which teachers rightly have to the work they do.

Establishing a Peer Support Group

This section is based on the practical experiences of one of the authors. He was instrumental in establishing a training programme for 15 PSG facilitators within a consortia of schools in Birmingham. The following practical guide gives the bare bones of a process which can be used by a PSG co-ordinator/facilitator in the initial stages of preparing the ground for the establishment of a PSG in school. We stress the importance of the facilitator's role in negotiating the direction and purposes of the PSG with senior management as well as PSG group members. Without this communication such a group might not fit easily within the institutional setting. A more detailed programme can be found in Mead (1991), Wallace and Mead (1991) and Mead (1992).

The PSG and what it can do

The PSG can be either a formal or informal grouping of school staff meeting to identify and tackle concerns that individual members of the group may have about their professional working lives. The size of the group may vary from two to ten. The group could run on a self-help basis or be the focus for helping staff to acquire expertise if they are not part of the group.

The tasks that a PSG might tackle will be numerous but broadly within the following headings:

- individual staff concerns about all aspects of school life – including stress management;
- academic and curriculum development for pupils and staff;
- classroom skills for pupils and staff;
- communication skills for pupils and staff;
- behaviour management skills;
- community development;
- administrative tasks.

This list is by no means exhaustive and readers, whether senior management, junior staff or departmental head, will identify their own concerns. We believe that almost any educational issue can be addressed by a PSG.

A PSG is effective because it tackles concerns that are relevant and shared by school staff. In discussing these concerns within the group solutions are put forward and then acted upon. The processes need be no more complicated if based on a viable form of social communication.

How to get started

In the author's programme, the basic approach to the establishment of PSGs was that of Self Organised Learning or SOL. (Thomas and Harri-Augstein, 1985; Harri-Augstein and Thomas, 1991). It was felt to be the approach most suited to PSGs as it engendered both personal learning and the organisational framework outlined earlier. Within the SOL it is necessary to identify the **purpose** of a project, what **methods** a group will use to achieve their purpose, what **outcomes** they expect from these strategies, and how they will **review** the process they have used. The planning and review process will allow PSG members to develop a positive approach and to reflect on courses of action taken by the group; thus actions are a powerful tool for enhancing professional development and awareness. This develops the group's capacity to learn how to function as a group within the context of school life as well as to take on tasks which generally improve the effectiveness of its members.

The rest of the chapter will ask readers – or potential group facilitators/co-ordinators – to define their own **purpose**, **methods**, **outcomes** and **review** processes in a series of tasks. The intention here is to use some of the features of a SOL approach to help a facilitator to set up a PSG project in school and prepare a plan to be put to possible group members and senior staff in the school. Beyond this planning stage a similar approach may be used by the facilitator to help the PSG determine its major tasks and functions.

The process of actually writing these down is a learning process in itself in that it will allow readers to share their ideas with others. Here we encourage readers to rehearse the development of a 'possible plan', in order to become more familiar with the process features of PSG development. It is necessary to bear in mind that in working with the group the purposes and methods identified below may need to be modified in the light of actual PSG discussion. Ideally, as facilitators, readers would share these activities with PSG members and in doing so it is intended that all staff involved in the process will have a sense of ownership of the work. This in turn should lead to a commitment to the project's success.

Defining a purpose

What is the purpose behind establishing a PSG in your school? What role would a PSG play in your school? What concerns would it take on board? Is this role in conflict with any other mechanism already in place in your school?

It is essential to ask why it is necessary for a PSG to be established in your school. A need must be identified. We would suggest that the purpose of a PSG would be to allow the sharing of ideas, where the joint construction of a problem and potential solutions lead to the development of group values. The sharing of perceptions at the level of **purposes** serves to reduce uncertainty and conflict which often emanate from a discussion which focuses solely on actions to be carried out.

In order to help you with the first task we offer the following guidelines.

(1) Purposes should be determined before associated actions are agreed; i.e. tasks/actions are subordinated to purposes.

(2) Establishing purposes allows you to remain reflective about the overall rationale for the work and not to be task driven. It gives an opportunity to define your own level of 'support' within the group and what that might entail.

(3) Purposes help with the formulation of desirable, potential outcomes and allow you to check for quality.

(4) Purposes can help negotiation with senior management in establishing the PSG. It is important to try to ensure that PSG purposes harmonise with the institution's policy on professional development and its general developmental plan.

When actually writing down your purposes it is important to remember that:

- purposes that are jointly formulated and explicitly stated make group consensus more likely and help avoid the possibility of hidden agendas. These should be open to modification through group discussion;
- purposes are ideal statements, hopeful achievements;
- there can be more than one purpose for a PSG or a project that a PSG initiates.

TASK 1
Use the orientation provided above to formulate the purposes a PSG might serve in your school.

What methods will you use?
Now you know why you want or need a PSG, how will you set it up? You will need to address most of the following questions and reflect on their significance to your own school.

- Who will be part of the PSG?
- Will the PSG be a self-help group or offer help to other staff? For example, staff working in a specialist area or developing school policy.
- How big will the group be?
- How will you best reflect the relevant experience of school staff?
- How will you integrate your PSG into present school practice?
- How will you engage the active interest and support of senior management?

- How will you actively develop the trust of colleagues?
- How will you run effective meetings?
- How do you communicate the role of the PSG to colleagues?
- How will you address the issue of confidentiality?
- How will you ascertain the core values of the group?
- What criteria will you use to answer the above?

By answering some of these questions you will be able to define the way you work before doing anything. This will help you understand the process and communicate your intentions clearly to other staff and senior management. This is essential if you are to attempt to negotiate into existence a PSG within directed time. You will then have begun to define your methods through creating working strategies.

TASK 2
Outline the methods you would use to establish a PSG in your school.

What outcomes do you expect from a PSG?
Having established your **purposes** and **methods** you are now in the position of being able to predict some expected outcomes of your work with a PSG. What do you hope the PSG will achieve for individual staff and for the whole school? For individual staff a PSG could be a way of:

- sharing good practice;
- stress reduction;
- increasing self-esteem;
- lessening any feelings of isolation;
- developing means and feelings of mutual support;
- increasing staff awareness of perceived difficulties;
- gaining ownership of their own problems and increasing personal effectiveness in relationships and work tasks.

For the whole school expected outcomes could include:

- an increased consistency of policy implementation;
- the development of a cohesive staff unit;
- better behaved children;
- more effective learners;
- improvements in policy and practice.

The process by which a PSG works will allow any expected outcomes to be shared. The effects that the work of a PSG has on individual staff or whole school should not be a surprise, as expected outcomes should be clearly stated before any projects are initiated.

TASK 3
What would you expect a PSG in your school to achieve?

How will you review the work of the PSG?
Once established, how will a PSG sustain itself? We suggest that a process of review is essential for PSGs to become and remain effective.

- What needs to be reviewed?
- Who will conduct any of the review procedures?
- How often will reviews take place?
- What administrative procedures will the PSG use for:

    - documentation and recording of meetings; these make a vital contribution to the group's ability to review its products and process;
    - budgeting;
    - resourcing;
    - monitoring and evaluation;
    - internal and external communication?

- What criteria will you set to evaluate the effectiveness of the PSG? It could include:

    - the number of staff using the PSG as a resource;
    - the success of support as perceived by the staff asking for it;
    - how staff feel about the role of the PSG within the school, and the perceived effectiveness of its efforts to complete tasks and projects.

It will be necessary for the PSG to review the process of its own formation and any of its projects, on a regular basis. This will ensure that:

(1) It remains clear about its own purposes, even if they should change.
(2) The PSG is able to facilitate change in staff and school without threat.
(3) It is able to engender trust amongst colleagues.

(4)   It is seen as a supportive mechanism, working within the whole school ethos and policy making process.

The review process has elements of personal development which allow time for reflection. This in turn engenders the sharing and self-organised learning process mentioned earlier.

TASK 4
Now, attempt to clarify any review procedures you think are necessary for your PSG.

It is worthwhile spending some time reflecting on what you have written for the tasks and what the major learning points have been up to this point. If possible share these tasks with a colleague, explaining what you have done, and why.

Timeline
After you have reviewed your plans, attempt to time budget them. A quick way to do this is to draw a line divided into weeks, months or terms. Plot onto the line all the factors involved in your plan to establish a PSG, such as negotiation time with senior management, PSG planning meetings, PSG meetings (see, for example, Figure 8.2).

Constructing a Timeline is a further way of sharing information with staff. It is also a powerful tool when negotiating the establishment of the PSG with senior management.

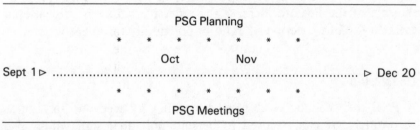

Figure 8.2   A Timeline

TASK 5
Construct your own timeline over a period of a school year

We suggest that you try and identify the dates of establishing your PSG, including your methods, when expected outcomes will happen and review-by dates. It would also help if you were able to attempt to include a project that your PSG might develop through PSG meetings. A further useful communicative act at this point would be to write up the outcomes of the previous sections in the form of a brief proposal to discuss with senior management.

As you move into your implementation phase and begin the process of setting your group up, you should bear in mind that your overall aim is to establish an open, collaborative and democratic group. The principles outlined earlier in this section which helped you identify a suitable PSG project (the negotiation of purposes, methods and outcomes) should be used to direct and review the life of your group.

The benefits of a PSG have already been outlined in previous sections and now you have established the reason for the existence of a PSG in your school you will want to get down to the business of putting it into operation. What a PSG does depends on its purpose, but a fundamental part of its function will be to allow staff to share the variety of educational concerns outlined earlier and in so doing:

● improve their practice;
● reduce stress;
● build up a sense of team/group work;
● raise awareness of issues and be more pro-active and assertive;
● show that problems and concerns can be adequately tackled without the need for 'expert' interventions;
● become more thoughtful practitioners.

It has been the intention of this chapter to introduce teachers to the task-oriented PSG, but we hope readers have also become aware of the role of the PSG to increase the reflective nature of educational work; a PSG as a period of calm in potentially turbulent waters.

Conclusion

A PSG then can be established according to need and developed accordingly. It can be used to benefit individual staff whilst also addressing organisational demands. Whatever its role, it has to address the issue of whether it is achieving its ultimate objective; that of allowing staff to feel better and more competent in relation to what they are doing at school. PSGs have the potential to improve the quality of a teacher's professional life through being able to share information with colleagues on an organisational level. Staff can receive individual guidance and also devise their own solutions to perceived concerns instead of solutions being imposed by 'experts'. In so doing they may develop an increased level of social companionship. This in turn can develop into a sense of emotional support that, combined with self-help strategies, establishes and maintains self-esteem that has been identified as crucial to the reduction of stress and the increased effectiveness of teacher performance.

References

Allington, T., Cooper, C. L. and Reynolds, P. (1989) 'Counselling in the Workplace: The Post Office Experience', *The Psychologist*, **2** (9), pp. 384–388.

Assistant Masters and Mistresses Association (1986) *A Review of the Research into the Primary Causes of Stress among Teachers*.

Argyle, M. (1991) *Co-operation: The Basis of Sociability*. London: Routledge.

Argyris, C. and Schon, D. (1987) *Theory and Practice: Increasing Professional Effectiveness*. New York: Holt Rinehart & Winston.

Borg, M. G. and Riding, R. J. (1991) 'Occupational Stress and Satisfaction in Teaching', *British Educational Research Journal*, **17** (3), pp. 263–281.

Caplan, G. and Killilea, M. (eds) (1976) *Support Systems and Mutual Help: Multidisciplinary Explorations*. New York: Grune & Stratton, Inc.

Cohen, L. and Manion, L. (1989) *Research Methods in Education* (3rd ed). London: Routledge.

Collins, T. and Bruce, T. (1984) *Staff Support and Staff Training*. London: Tavistock Publications.

Cox, T., Boot, N. and Harrison, S. (1988) 'Stress in Schools: An Organisational Perspective', *Work and Stress*, **2** (4), pp. 353–62.

Dockar-Drysdale, B. (1973) 'Problems Arising in the Communication of Stress', in *Consultation in Child Care*. London: Longmans.

Dunham, J. (1984) *Stress in Teaching*. London: Croom-Helm.

Education Service Advisory Committee (1990) *Managing Occupational Stress: A Guide for Managers and Teachers in the Schools Sector*. Health and Safety Executive.

Fiske, A. P. (1991) 'The Cultural Relativity of Selfish Individualism: Anthropological Evidence that Humans are Inherently Sociable', in Clark, M. S. (ed) *Prosocial Behaviour*. California: Sage.

Gray, H. and Freeman, A. (1987) *Teaching without Stress*. London: Paul Chapman Ltd.

GRIDS (1988) *GRIDS: Guidelines for Review and Internal Development in Schools*. Secondary School Handbook (2nd ed). London: Longman.

Hanko, G. (1985) *Special Needs in Ordinary Classrooms*. London: Basil Blackwell Ltd.

Harri-Augstein, E. S. and Thomas, L. F. (1991) *Learning Conversations: The Self-Organised Way to Personal and Organisational Growth*. London: Routledge.

Hargreaves, D. H., Hopkins, D., Leask, M., Connolly, J. and Robinson, P. (1990) *Planning for School Development: Advice to Governors, Headteachers and Teachers*. London: DES.

Johnstone, M. (1989) *Stress in Teaching: An Overview of Research*. The Scottish Council for Research in Education.

Kearney, D. and Turner, K. (1987) 'Peer Support and Stress Management for Headteachers', *Educational Psychology in Practice*, **29** (2), pp. 146–152.

Killilea, M. (1976) 'Mutual Help Organisations: Interpretations in the Literature', in Caplan, G. and Killilea, M. (eds) *Support Systems and Mutual Help: Multidisciplinary Explorations*. New York: Grune & Stratton, Inc.

Klein, E. B. (1979) 'Manifestations of Transference in Small Training Groups', in Lawrence, W. G. (ed) *Exploring Individual and Group Boundaries: A Tavistock Open Systems Approach*. London: John Wiley & Sons Ltd.

Kyriacou, C. and Sutcliffe, J. (1978) 'Teacher Stress: Prevalence Sources and Symptoms', *British Journal of Educational Psychology*, 48, pp. 159–67.

Mead, C. (1991) *A City-Wide Evaluation of PSG Training*. Birmingham Local Education Authority. Available from Education Department, Margaret Street, Birmingham B3 3BU.

Mead, C. (1992) MAPPER: A Formative Evaluation of a Project Management Resource. MEd Dissertation, Faculty of Education, Birmingham University.

Myers, M. and Cherry, C. (1990) *MAPPER Manual*. Available from IODA, 203 Rugby Road, Leamington Spa, Warwicks.

Myers, M., Cherry, C., Timmins, P., Brzezinska, H., Miller, P. and Willey, R. (1989) 'System Supplied Information (SSI): How to Assess Needs and Plan Effectively within Schools/Colleges', *Educational Psychology in Practice*, **5** (2), pp. 91–96.

Nelson-Jones, R. (1991) *Lifeskills: A Handbook*. London: Cassell.

Newton, P. and Levinson, D. (1973) 'The Work Group within the Organisation', *Psychiatry*, Vol 36, May, pp. 115–142.

Nichols, K. and Jenkinson, J. (1991) *Leading a Support Group*. London: Chapman and Hall.

Oja, S. and Smulyan, L. (1989) *Collaborative Action Research: Developmental Approach*. London: Falmer.

Paquette, M. (1987) 'Voluntary Collegial Support Groups for Teachers', *Educational Leadership*, **45** (3), pp. 36–39.

Reason, P. and Rowan, J. (eds) (1981) *Human Inquiry, A Sourcebook of New Paradigm Research*. Chichester: Wiley.

Reason, P. (ed) (1988) *Human Inquiry in Action: Developments in New Paradigm Research*. London: Sage.

Rees, F. (1989) *Teacher Stress: An Exploratory Study*. National Foundation for Educational Research.

Santora, J. (1988) 'Professional Development: Tapping Departmental Potential', *English Journal*, 77 (4), pp. 45–46.

Schon, D. (1971) *Beyond the Stable State*. London: Penguin.

Skynner, R. (1989) 'An Experiment in Group Consultation with the Staff of a Comprehensive School', in Schlapobersky, J. R. (ed) *Institutes and How to Survive Them: Mental Health Training and Consultation*. London: Routledge.

Stringer, P., Stow, L., Hibbert, K., Powell, J. and Louw, E. (1992) 'Establishing Staff Consultation Groups in Schools', *Educational Psychology in Practice*, **2**, pp. 87–96.

Stronge, J.H. and Helm, V.M. (1991) *Evaluating Professional Support Personnel in Education*. London: Sage.

Thies-Sprinthall, L.M. and Gerler, E.R. (Jr) (1990) 'Support Groups for Novice Teachers', *Journal of Staff Development*, **11** (4), pp. 18–22.

Thomas, L.F. and Harri-Augstein, E.S. (1985) *Self-Organised Learning: Foundations for a Conversational Science of Psychology*. London: Routledge & Kegan Paul.

Timmins, P. and Dunkley, D. (1990) 'Steps Towards a Partnership with Parents: A Self-Organised Learning Perspective', *Educational and Child Psychology*, **7** (2), pp. 61–70.

Wallace, F. and Mead, C. (1991) An Evaluation of PSG Training: Sparkbrook/Sparkhill Consortium. Available from Birmingham Psychological Service Central, 74 Balden Road, Harborne, Birmingham B32.

Wills, T.A. (1991) 'Social Support and Interpersonal Relationships', in Clark, M.S. (ed) *Prosocial Behaviour*. California: Sage.

Wragg, E. (1987) 'Teacher Appraisal', *Scottish Educational Review*, **19** (2), pp. 76–85.

Zins, J.E., Maher, C.A., Murphy, J.J. and Wess, B.P. (1988) 'The Peer Support Group: A Means to Facilitate Professional Development', *School Psychology Review*, **17** (1), pp. 138–146.

Index